THE LOST ART OF BEING SAVED

A SIX-WEEK JOURNEY INTO GREATER INTIMACY WITH GOD

ALISTAIR KENT

The Small Print

The Loving Note

Dedicated to my
pastoring partner,
footballing friend
and wonderful wife,
Kate Kent.

The Contents

The Route Planner

DIAGRAMS AND ILLUSTRATIONS play a significant part in this book, so if you like to visualise things more you can see the journey ahead on this spread.

WEEK 1: POSITIONED FOR INTIMACY

When we accept Jesus into our hearts by faith, we take him in his fullness. Our spirits are revived and we enter into a life with Father God where he adopts us as his children. And because his Spirit is inside us we take on his divine nature.

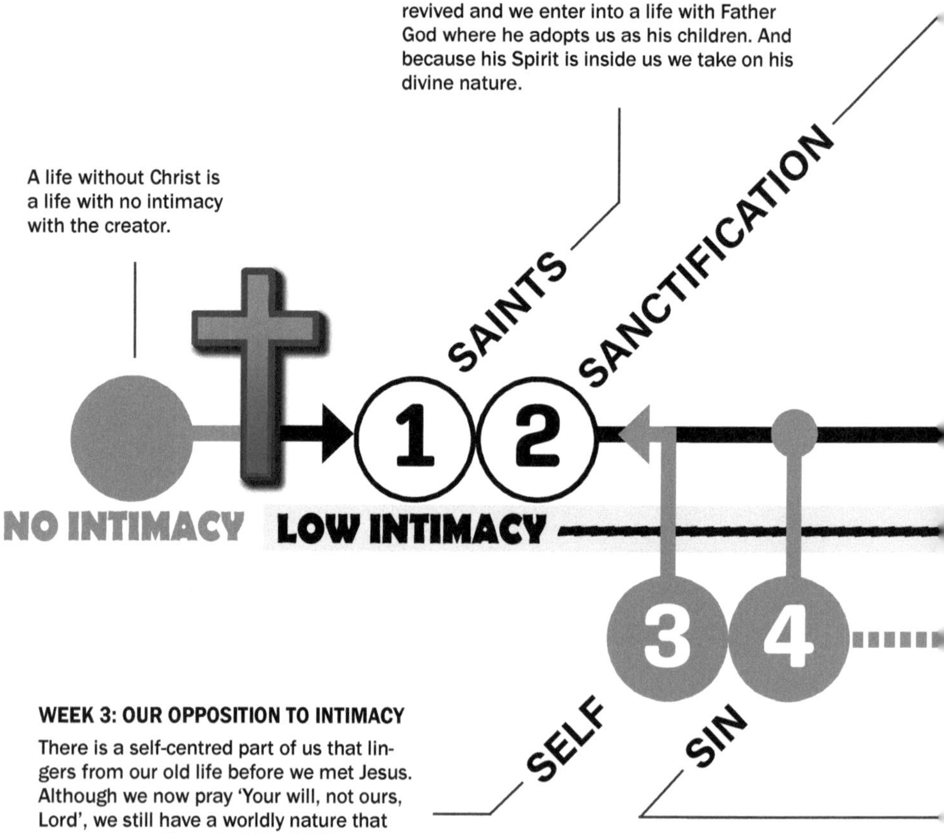

WEEK 3: OUR OPPOSITION TO INTIMACY

There is a self-centred part of us that lingers from our old life before we met Jesus. Although we now pray 'Your will, not ours, Lord', we still have a worldly nature that opposes everything that the Spirit wants to do in us and through us.

WEEK 2: THE JOURNEY INTO INTIMACY

We weren't saved just to go to heaven someday; we have a journey ahead of us that continues until we take our last breath. It's a pathway that leads into the presence of God, and we get there by thinking more holy thoughts that in turn lead to holy actions.

WEEK 5: THE DOORWAY TO INTIMACY

Walking with God as our Saviour is great, but working for God as our Lord and Master is vital if we are going to enter the fullness of a relationship that he wants to have with us.

WEEK 6: OUR WALK OF INTIMACY

The final phase of intimacy with God is found in walking in step with the Spirit, being led and guided by him. This is where we hear God's voice clearly and experience a deep and continual fellowship with God.

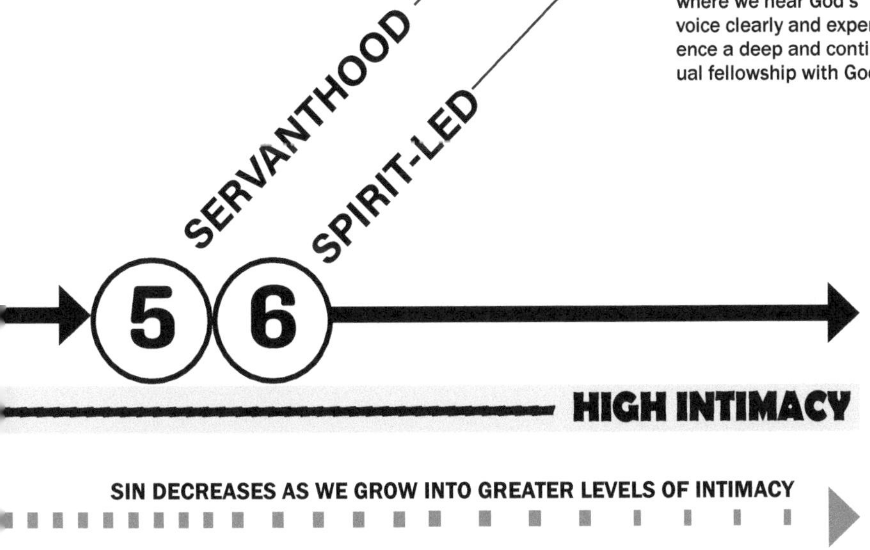

WEEK 4: OUR BARRIER TO INTIMACY

To be tempted within our selfish nature is not wrong, but when we choose to act according to it we sin. These wrong thoughts or actions have to be forgiven for us to continue in our journey of intimacy with God.

The Background

After 10 years of pastoring our local church in a suburb south of Nottingham, Kate and I were due to go on a sabbatical. Unfortunately the plan was to go in 2020, the year that saw the invasion of Covid. Lockdowns were initiated. Plans were put on ice.

As the year progressed it turned out that the worldwide virus wasn't going to be as short-lived as we'd hoped. The epidemic became a pandemic. Plans were shelved.

Into 2021 and everything was still up in the air: fluctuating case counts, new strains and various restrictions.

Finally, though, 2022 brought back some kind of normality, so plans were made for a three-month break from the day-to-day running of the church.

Whereas Kate can slip into holiday mode at the flick of a switch, I find myself having to prepare not just practically but mentally too. I spent months getting myself ready for being totally hands-off.

We'd planned several things during our time away. In the mix were a couple of vacations (one on home soil and one abroad), visits to other churches, and a three-week retreat on a remote part of the west coast of Scotland for some studying and writing.

I was excited to get this underway and start writing a new leadership course that God had led me to put together. What I didn't realise was that my timing wasn't his timing. My planned writing schedule experienced a heavenly hijacking.

At the beginning of our time away I started getting loads of thoughts around the subject of intimacy with God that I needed to write down. And for every thought came an illustration that I had to sketch. I thought I'd just spend a week getting everything down, then I'd get back to my original plan. But one week turned into two, two into three, and by the end of the sabbatical virtually all three months were filled with the musings, concepts and teachings found in this book.

Interestingly, after making the decision to postpone my scheduled plans and pursue God's leading, the next night I was blue-lighted into the local emergency department. (I say 'local'; being in rural Scotland it was 45 minutes away—and it looked more like a youth centre than a hospital!) My heart was racing like a steam train, clocking up to 180 beats per minute. Thankfully it started calming down after a couple of hours, and I was then kept in overnight for observations. The ECG recorded activity known as atrial fibrillation.

The doctor on duty that night (definitely not a youth worker: he had a stethoscope round his neck) assured me that I hadn't had a heart attack and that I could leave. That was it—until the next night, which was pretty much a repeat of the previous episode. Another ambulance ride ensued. I'll say more about this later on.

You may call the decision to write this book and the ensuing health issues a mere coincidence—or maybe of no relevance—but I call it opposition. Spiritual opposition.

This book wasn't my idea. My name's on the front cover because I wrote it, but I don't see that I authored it. I believe I've heard from God, and in the process have faithfully transferred as much as I can from my spirit onto these pages.

I don't know exactly how God will use this book, but I do know that he told me to put any profits from it into our church's building project fund. So by buying this copy—as well as hopefully benefiting from the content—you'll be contributing towards improving our facility and in turn helping us to better serve our surrounding community.

The Introduction

BEING SAVED

Picture the closing scenes in the movie *Titanic*. Rose (Kate Winslet) is floating in the middle of the Atlantic Ocean on a piece of debris from the not-so-indestructible vessel. She's been in the freezing waters for hours, void of all hope, when in the depth of the night a rescue lifeboat can be seen in the distance. A torch light sweeps the surface of the surrounding waters. Rose—probably close to hypothermia—doesn't have the energy to shout; but spotting a whistle on a dead man's life-jacket she takes the plunge into the icy waters towards it.

Anxious that the rescuers are now passing her by, she musters all the oxygen she can from her starved lungs to blow into the whistle. The rescue boat (almost giving up on finding anyone alive in the carnage) hears the high-pitched SOS call and gets a visual on the damsel in extreme distress. She's thrown a rope, she's pulled on board... She's saved!

She's not fully restored to her pre-ship-sinking condition, but she's saved from her own failing ability to stay alive. The seamen take her, along with other survivors, to the eventual safety and security of dry land where she will finally be saved, with no more pain or suffering.

In a broad sense, we can use this illustration to chart a course for our own personal salvation.

Just like the fall of man affects every human being irrespective of age, status or health, the Titanic too was a leveller. Into the deep dark sea of despair it tossed both the hired hands and the wealthy they were serving.

Whether we realised it or not, we too were void of hope, clinging onto whatever we could to get us through our troubled waters. But then, out of the blue, the searchlight of Jesus shone directly on us. We called out to him to rescue us. He obliged. We were saved!

He came to us as our Saviour. And he's going to return a second time as King. He will put an end to all sin and suffering and make all things new again, as was intended in the very beginning of creation. Our salvation experience will then be complete. Just as Rose found full salvation when she reached the security of dry land, we too will eventually set foot in a new heaven on a new earth when we receive our new supernatural, glorified, everlasting bodies. Humankind will then pick up again with God's interrupted eternal plan of worshipping him, whilst managing the affairs of his Kingdom as he sees fit.

But what about this current phase of salvation we're in now before he returns? What about *being* saved? What's that all about? What are we meant to do? What's expected of us? Do we even need to do anything? And what part does Christ play in it all—if anything?

That's the general terrain we'll be journeying through in this book.

VARYING DEGREES

Right now, across the entire world, every Christian has one thing in common: Christ—the hope of glory. He's living simultaneously inside each and every person who has been born again of the Spirit of God. That's amazing!

However, even though that one heavenly common denominator is in each of us, there's a huge myriad of expressions towards God being played out from one believer to the next. I'm not referring to different personalities and gifts that we all have, but the different degrees of spirituality we have in our 'being-saved-ness'.

This phenomenon is not just witnessed on a global scale; you can see it by zooming right in to your own local church. You could even go further and focus on only a small handful of random Christians; the chances are that you'll have one person who is backsliding, one who is on fire for God, and the others will be somewhere in between. Some are in tune with the Spirit, some are confused by the Spirit; some are living under their circumstances and some are living above them; some have faith to raise the dead and some don't believe that God even heals today.

If we're all getting different experiences from our salvation, then we must all be doing different things! But what if there was one main thing that we should all be doing? What if, amongst all the 31,102 verses in the Bible, there was actually a standout goal in our sights that most people are missing?

TOP PRIORITIES

There are two particular scriptures that talk of priorities.

When asked what the greatest commandment of all was, Jesus replied in ***Matthew 22:37-38 (NIVUK), "Love the Lord your God with all your heart and with all your soul and with all your mind. This is the first and greatest commandment."*** Basically Jesus is saying, 'Give me your everything; go all-in with your Christianity; abandon all, and find the true meaning of life.'

Then, in his Sermon on the Mount, Jesus is teaching about the ills of worry and about not focusing on material necessities. He instructs the crowds to ***"seek first his kingdom and his righteousness, and all these things will be given to you as well" (Matthew 6:33 NIVUK).*** 'Pursue me!', he's saying again, 'and you'll receive everything you need—both spiritually *and* materially.'

The 'art of being saved' is not about the latest ideas and strategies from some great Christian thought leaders. These can be very valuable; we need cutting-edge prophetic people to speak into the Church at this time. But the clue to the hope this book provides is in the full title: *The Lost Art of Being Saved.*

Something we've lost, by definition, is something we've had all along. That something is *someone*. His name is Jesus. Now we've not lost Jesus *per se*; he's inside us by his Spirit. What we've lost is the art of relating to him.

That may not be anything you haven't heard before, and it probably doesn't get your spiritual veins pumping with the blood of Jesus, but there's always more to our relationship with God than we think. As we start to get underneath what it means to pursue him for a real, authentic relationship of increasing intimacy, my desire is that you will receive both the depths of wisdom and the heights of revelation as you engage with different parts of this book that the Spirit particularly draws you to.

Now I don't want to judge inappropriately, but in some church circles it seems that *Jesus being the centre* is a somewhat relegated theme because *reaching the lost* is of paramount importance—after all, the days are short and Jesus is returning! We can be so busy being on trend, relevant, and seeker-friendly that we neglect the power source we need to achieve that. I want to nail my colours to the mast here: I'm passionate about the lost. I'm passionate about unsaved people coming to church and engaging in our systems and programmes, but we can't afford to sever the source of our being in the pursuit of proclaiming Christ to others. We can't let the busyness of our lives supersede the true business of God: being in relationship with him.

The central theme of this book is *intimacy*: a pursuit towards God that reveals increasingly greater levels of access to Christ in your life, and the flow of love, faith and hope that spills out from that.

THE PENDING ADVENTURE

Over the next six weeks I invite you to journey with me as we head out together on a fresh discovery mission where we'll re-evaluate our priorities and re-centre God in our lives.

The first seven days will see us laying some foundations, making sure we understand who we are in Christ and how we've been created to function.

In Week Two we'll look ahead to what God wants for us, seeing what is achievable, and getting a fresh vision for all that we can accomplish in him. We'll focus in on what it means to be fruitful and the thrill of pleasing God.

But no one said it was going to be easy! Even Jesus said that we'd experience troubles in this life. Equally, there are plenty of difficulties that we bring on ourselves, without thinking about those from outside forces—like the world and the devil. All of this and more is discussed in the third week.

Then in Week Four we'll look sin straight in the eye, exposing it for what it is. We'll be looking at the cause of it, seeing the effect of it and starting a journey of minimising its potential in our lives.

Understanding more fully what it means to follow not just a Saviour, but a Lord—a King, a Master, a Ruler—that's our pursuit in Week Five.

Then, as we conclude in Week Six, we'll start to flesh out some of the practical ways we get to experience and enjoy this new way to be human that we've been called to.

HOW IT ALL WORKS

Each day you'll be invited to take a few minutes to read a particular aspect or truth based on the current weekly focus. Following that, there are some questions to ponder—these will expand your thinking and challenge you to bring some application, especially in light of the stark reality presented in ***James 1:22 (NLT), "don't just listen to God's word. You must do what it says. Otherwise, you are only fooling yourselves."***

Although this book is clearly divided into days and weeks, there are a few strands of truth that have been weaved into different sections at different times. You'll also find some repetition. You'll also find some repetition (sorry, I couldn't stop myself). This is all intentional to help you build on concepts, and to cement the important themes that we'll be focusing on.

My writings are certainly not in depth. Rather, the approach I've taken is to cover as many general aspects of *being saved* as I can in the space I have available. (One of my self-rejected titles for this book was *The Idiot's Guide to Being a Christian*, but the derogatory connotations outweighed the catchy title.) Hopefully my writings are something that any believer, of any level of maturity and experience, can pick up and find inspiration for their next step in their walk with God.

For the newer Christian reading this, there's a glossary of the most-used terms in the back of the book (pages 245-251). If that's you, it may be useful to go there next and familiarise yourself with some of them. For the more learned believer, I pray that you will see the age-old truths of scripture in a brand new light—especially as we connect it all to the intimacy that God calls us to in him!

I produced an initial small run of this book for our church, and I also decided to preach a six-week sermon series based on each of the six sections. The book then became a great way of building on the Sunday teachings during the week as each member went deeper by reading the relevant chapters. Some even took it upon themselves to discuss the week's focus in their small groups, by each bringing their answer to one of the questions at the end of each chapter.

Most people read the book as suggested, on a daily basis. Some, however, decided to read it all the way through and then went back a second time to digest further. A few lagged a little, but most found it really easy to catch up with the rest of the congregation because of the short chapters.

The way you engage with this book doesn't actually matter that much. What matters is that it connects you to your heavenly Father at a new level. That might be through a series of small steps, or through a radical moment of revelation and transformation.

ON YOUR MARKS...

Wherever you are on this chartered course of *being saved*, my prayer for you is that you engage with this book in a spirit of humility, wanting to learn more from the greatest teacher ever: the Holy Spirit. My desire is that you'll be amazed by what God can do—and will do—in your life. So why don't you partner with me in that pursuit from the outset and pray this prayer...

"Lord God, creator of heaven and earth, King of my heart and lover of my soul, I come to you right now and present my whole self to you: spirit, soul and body. This book has landed in my hands by one means or another. You know how; you know why. You saw this moment before the beginning

of time, and you know what words I need to change me so that I can be used as a vessel of goodness to bring you glory.

"Help me, Holy Spirit, each day to take at least a few minutes to engage with the truths I read, then continue to speak to me as you see fit so that we can venture into Kingdom living like never before. May the print on these pages speak into the depths of my soul; may dreams surface and revelation flow; may my heart be drawn to yours like never before as we enter into my unknown and your known. Set me free, set me alight and set me on course to a life of greater intimacy with you.

"In the almighty, all-powerful name of your precious Son, Jesus Christ, I pray. Amen."

The perfect God
came to live in your
imperfect being.

WEEK 1

Positioned for intimacy: SAINTS

THE NEW LIFE

Jesus came not solely to forgive us our sins—that was a means to an end. What was the end? Life. But in the infamous words of Mr Spock spoken in the 1987 *Star Trek* parody song, "It's life, Jim, but not as we know it" (okay, I'm showing my age now!). We previously only knew the life that pulled us down, that made impossible demands on us, that dished out disappointments, depression and delusions.

Now we get to live the new life. We're still in the old world—until Jesus comes again and makes all things new—but we have full access to journey through God's roadmap of life with him steering our course. He guides us in the right paths, he provides for us as we travel, he protects us from harm and he puts on heaven's playlist for us to worship along the way.

The world can still pull us in the opposite direction to the destiny God has for us, but we are no longer ruled by our own desires; the Spirit of God has now become our internal satnav.

THE DEVIL'S INTERVENTION

There's one other big problem in our journey of life: the devil. He has lost his grip on us, thanks to Christ defeating him in the grave, so he has to resort to lies and deceit. Satan used to be in close relationship with God; he was head of heaven's worship department. But he got proud. He wanted to be like God. (Warning: be godly, but don't try and be God!) As a result of his rebellion, Satan was cast down out of heaven onto the earth.

He can't directly harm you, but he can lead you into harm's way. And by this most would think about physical harm, whether that be attack or illness. But the greatest harm he can afflict you with is his lies. Specifically, to lie to you about your identity in Christ. He wants you to spiritually self-harm in this area.

His lies go something like this: "You're worthless. You messed up. Again. Call yourself a Christian? You hypocrite!"

It's his one last attempt to derail your faith, or at least to quarantine you in guilt and condemnation. But the Bible says that there is no condemnation for those in Christ Jesus (Romans 8:1)! Who are you going to believe, the devil or God?

When the Apostle Paul wrote letters to the churches he had previously planted he addressed the believers as *saints*. Could they still sin? Yes. Did they still sin? You bet. Not least the Corinthian church, who were meddling in a whole bunch of carnal behaviours, yet Paul still started his somewhat harsh letter, ***"To the church of God which is at Corinth, to those who are sanctified in Christ Jesus, called to be saints, with all who in every place call on the name of Jesus Christ our Lord, both theirs and ours:"* (*1 Corinthians 1:2 NKJV,*** emphasis mine).

Just as you can't be both light *and* darkness, you can't be both a sinner *and* a saint. ***Romans 5:8 (NLT)*** declares that ***"God showed his great love for us by sending Christ to die for us while we were still sinners."*** Note the word *were*. Past tense. We were sinners; now we are saints.

'Saint' means *holy one*. That's who you are. Let that sink in...

Jesus told a parable about a lost son who left the family home to *go it alone*. After squandering his inheritance through partying and rich living, he finally came to his senses and, in humility, returned home to his father. Although he totally messed up, he was still a son and the father looked upon him in that way. Not like a broken failure, but as a returning child. Take note: your identity has nothing to do with your behaviour.

Here's another truth worth remembering: you became a Christian not by worth, but by birth. You were birthed into his Kingdom. When you were born again you became a saint. A holy one. That's who you are. That's how God sees you. That's how he wants you to see yourself.

You're adopted as his child; you're a completely brand new creation in Christ Jesus; you were bought with a price; you're a partaker of God's divine nature; you hold great value. Yes, you still have the ability to sin, but you're not a sinner. You might currently be sinning a lot, but that's the old you. The new you, the redeemed you, is labelled *saint*. God doesn't put up with you in your sin; he delights in you in his holiness.

SINNING SAINTS

Let's make this absolutely clear, though: sin is still an issue. It can create a foothold in our lives, it can give access to the devil and it can hinder our intimacy with God (we'll be looking into this a lot more throughout Week 4), but it does not take away from who you are. You're not a sinner who occasionally has a few saintly moments. You're a saint who, on occasion, sins. Big difference.

And we can even take this up another level: *Who* you are is important, but *whose* you are is just as important—arguably even more. Why? Because being a saint can end up as a prideful, empty mantra, but continually remembering who gave you your saint status can keep you humble, whilst remaining in your undeserved but privileged position.

Listen, if you don't think you're worthy to speak with the Most High God, you won't. If you don't think God wants to show you great and mighty things, you won't position yourself to see them. If you don't think God has already given love and forgiveness to a wretched sinner like you, you won't experience them. We may be saved, but we still need to be transformed by the renewing of our minds.

In this first week we'll look into these real thoughts and issues. We'll use our position in Christ as the foundation for our pursuit of him. From that we'll see how our relationship with God works in practice, what it looks like and what can hinder it.

So with that introduction to this week's underlying theme, let's get going.

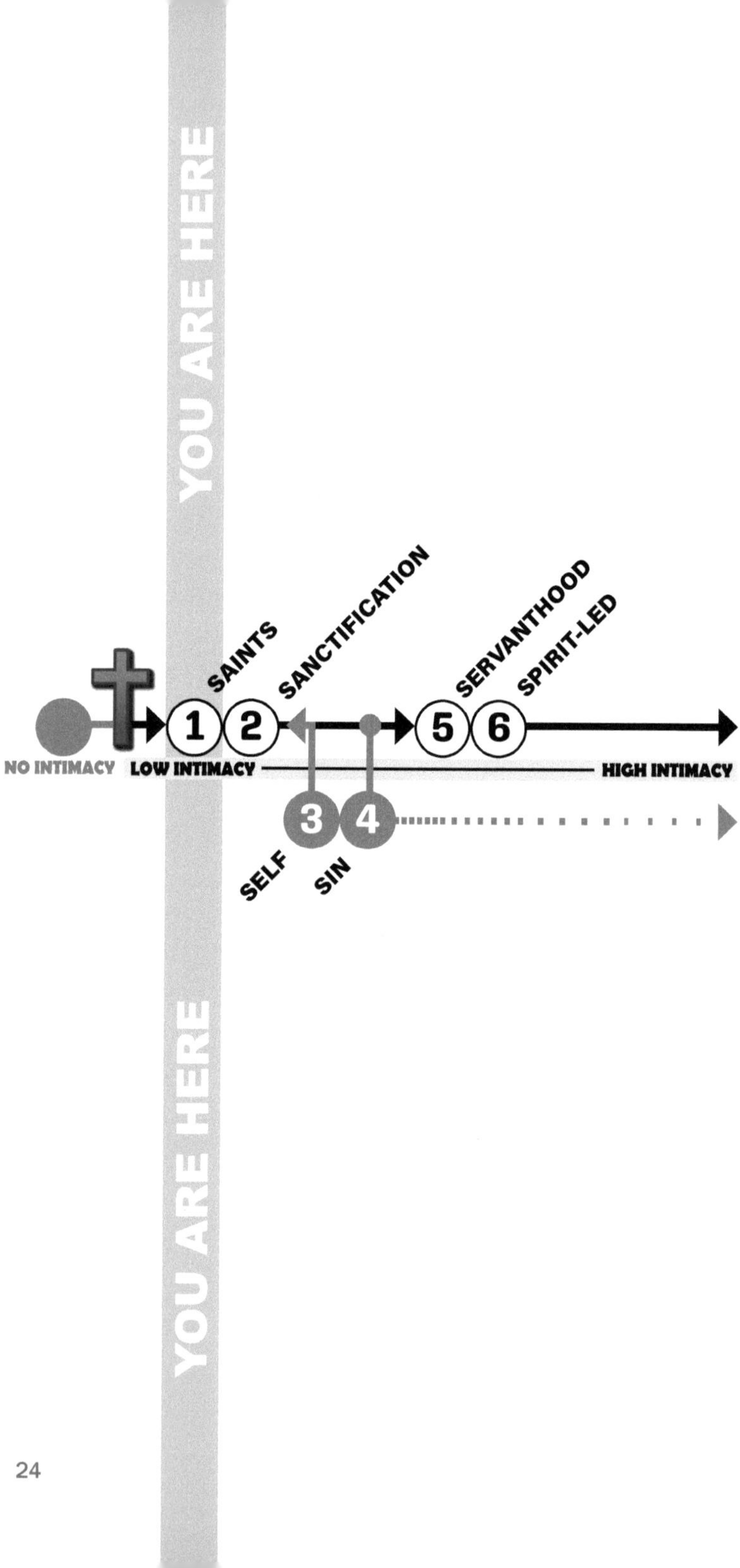
YOU ARE HERE
SAINTS
SANCTIFICATION
SERVANTHOOD
SPIRIT-LED
1
2
5
6
NO INTIMACY
LOW INTIMACY
HIGH INTIMACY
3
4
SELF
SIN
YOU ARE HERE

DAY 1

KNOWING GOD

IF I ASKED you, 'What is eternal life?', you might answer, 'a gift from God'. Well, you'd be right in that conclusion, but there's more to it.

You might expand, 'Eternal life is spending forever with God in heaven'. That would be true also—but only in part, because eternal life isn't just about the afterlife; it's about the here-and-now life. The moment you accepted Jesus Christ as your Lord and Saviour you received the free gift of eternal life. But even this doesn't paint the full picture.

Thankfully, there's a place in scripture that actually spells out a fuller answer for us. Let's jump there. ***John 17:3 (NLT), "And this is the way to have eternal life—to know you, the only true God, and Jesus Christ, the one you sent to earth."***

Did you catch that? That's a biblical definition of eternal life right there, all wrapped up in a small parcel of two words—even two syllables: to *know you*. Or, in context, to *know God* (still two syllables).

Eternal life is not just about living forever, but more about knowing God. Not just in the afterlife but right here, right now.

The original Greek word translated as *know* is *ginóskó*. It means 'to personally know with firsthand experience', and carries with it a depth of intimacy, even to the extent of sexual intercourse (yes, I went there). We can see the same word being used in ***Luke 1:34 (NKJV)*** when the virgin Mary responds to the angel's news that she'll conceive a child. She replied to the heavenly messenger, ***"How can this be, since I do not <u>know</u> a man?"*** (emphasis mine).

When we receive eternal life, we enter into a relationship. A relationship with the Creator of the cosmos. The lover of our souls. The One who gave up the life of his one and only Son so that we could be united with him. When Jesus died on the cross to take away the sins of mankind, he didn't do this so that we can spend everlasting life with him in heaven; he did it so that the intimate relationship between man and God could be restored on earth.

We were created to *ginóskó* God.

Sadly, many believers are associated with God by name only. Family and friends may know them as Christians, but they lack the fruit of a

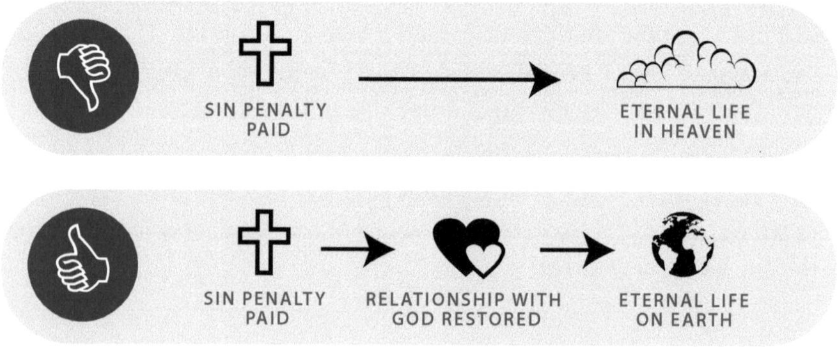

close relationship with God. They may profess to love God, but we're not called just to *love* him; we're called to be *in* love with him!

When the much-loved Queen Elizabeth II passed away in 2022, tens of thousands of people queued for up to 10 miles—some for over 20 hours—to file past the monarch's coffin and pay their respects. To travel to a congested capital and wait that long says something not just about the character of the Queen but also about the connectedness people had with her. And it wasn't just the people lining up in London; it was the millions who watched from further afield on their TV screens. The bond extended worldwide and was shared, not just by many of the 2.5 billion in the Commonwealth, but by multitudes across the globe who felt at least some kind of affinity to Her Majesty's life and legacy.

But here's the thing: whilst billions may have in some way felt connected, and tens of thousands travelled and queued to see the coffin, only a very small percentage actually *knew* the Queen personally. And even fewer knew her more intimately.

And that's the parallel we see today with Christians and Christ. Of all the believers in the world, how many are actually committed to the extent that it costs them their time and money even just to worship with others every Sunday? And how many of those could say they have an intimate, personal relationship with him?

Even sadder is the fact that millions of people claim to be Christian just because they live in a Christian nation, or maybe because they go to church every Christmas and Easter. The fact is that the only way to God is by having a relationship with Jesus Christ. In ***John 14:6 (NIVUK)*** Jesus said, ***"I am the way and the truth and the life. No one comes to the Father except through me."***

Putting it bluntly, if you take *Christ* out of being *Christ-ian* you're just left with being an 'Ian' (I appeal to the grace of all Ians out there to allow this analogy to make its full impact without causing any offence in your hearts).

So Christianity is about having a relationship with God, one that is not just by name but by experience. And not just a fleeting experience, but one that is constant, growing over time and deepening with affection.

Maybe you have been around church all your life; maybe you haven't been in church, but still pray to God occasionally; maybe you're part of another religion but still believe in the one and only true and living God. Whatever your situation, God knows you and sees you.

If something deep within your heart is open right now to believe that God loves you, wants the best for you and created you to be in relationship with him, then all you have to do is follow the instructions of ***Romans 10:9 (NLT): "If you openly declare that Jesus is Lord and believe in your heart that God raised him from the dead, you will be saved."***

QUESTIONS TO PONDER

- What does having eternal life right now look like to you?
- If you had to convince the jury in a court of law that you have a relationship with God, what evidence would you give?
- As with any relationship, it takes two to tango. How is your dance with the Lord? Are you holding him tightly or just gazing across the ballroom at him from time to time?
- Where have you strayed from God's love or drifted from his presence? What one thing can you put into practice from today that will bring you closer to God?

YESTERDAY'S SUMMARY: Eternal life is to know God intimately from the moment of being born again, not just waiting for the afterlife.

DAY 2

THREE-PART BEINGS

OF ALL THE truths in the Bible, I wish I had been taught this one a lot earlier than I was. When I learned what I'm going to summarise for you today, it clicked so many things into place. I pray it will help you, too. I believe it's a fundamental teaching that every Christian needs to grasp in order to live a victorious life and enter fully into the precious relationship that God wants us to have with him.

Look in the mirror. Who do you see? I'm guessing your answer might be something like 'me'. But just because you can't see something doesn't mean it's not there or it's not real. There's more to you than meets the eye! So I'll ask again: Who do you see?

Let's do some digging to get the right answers.

You're actually made up of three distinct parts: one visible and two invisible.

The Bible tells us in ***Genesis 1:27 (NLT)*** that ***"God created human beings in his own image."*** One of the mysteries of God is that he is a three-part being: Father, Son and Spirit (one being in three persons). So maybe it's not a surprise to us that we are made up of three parts as well. The Apostle Paul in his final greeting to the church at Thessalonica tells us what these three parts are: ***1 Thessalonians 5:23 (NLT)*** says, ***"may the God of peace make you holy in every way, and may your whole spirit and soul and body be kept blameless until our Lord Jesus Christ comes again"*** (emphasis mine).

Pay special attention to the order that the scripture lists these three parts: spirit first, then soul, lastly body. This is intentional. Our spirits are mentioned first because that's who we are! We're made in God's image, remember. And ***John 4:24*** says **God is Spirit**, therefore so are we!

If you only take away one thing from today's teaching, then grab a hold of this truth: You *are* a spirit; you *have* a soul; you *live* in a body. Rest this book upside down on your lap for a minute or two and just think about that...

Welcome back.

The Bible makes a wild but true statement. Brace yourself, here it is: ***2 Corinthians 5:17 (NLT)*** says ***"anyone who belongs to Christ has become a new person. The old life is gone; a new life has begun!"*** So what part of you became new? Let's find out.

When you asked Jesus into your life did your body change or start to look any different? No—so it wasn't your *body* that became new. After you were saved did your intellect suddenly change? For example, did you suddenly grasp the intricacies of quantum physics or understand a foreign language? No—so it wasn't your *soul* that became new. That just leaves your *spirit*. This is the part of you that was born again.

It's most commonly agreed by Bible scholars and teachers that the soul realm contains our mind, our will and our emotions—that's our intellect, our desires and our passions. (Note that your *mind* in the soul realm is different to your *brain* in your body. We'll cover this more later.) So when ***Romans 12:2*** talks about being *transformed* it's not talking about the spirit, because that's been completely made brand new. It's talking about your soul. How does that happen? By renewing it with the Word of God.

This is why ***James 1:21 (NLT)*** tells us to ***"humbly accept the word God has planted in your hearts, for it has the power to save your souls".*** And it's also the reason ***Proverbs 11:30 (NKJV)*** says, ***"he who wins souls is wise".***

The mind is the mediator between spirit and body. God has already transformed your spirit; the transformation of your body is yet to happen when Christ returns. So, in the meantime, he needs to focus on changing your soul. And that's where Satan knows he can best attack us.

Whoever has control of your soul has control over you. Satan can't go after your spirit because the all-powerful Spirit of Christ lives there. He can attack your body, but he'd rather attack your mind—your control centre.

Our bodies are the material part of us; it's the part we most commonly and easily identify with. And herein lies one of the greatest problems Christians face: navigating a physical world as a spiritual being. That's why ***2 Corinthians 5:7 (NIVUK)*** instructs us that the new way of living is to ***"live by faith, not by sight."***

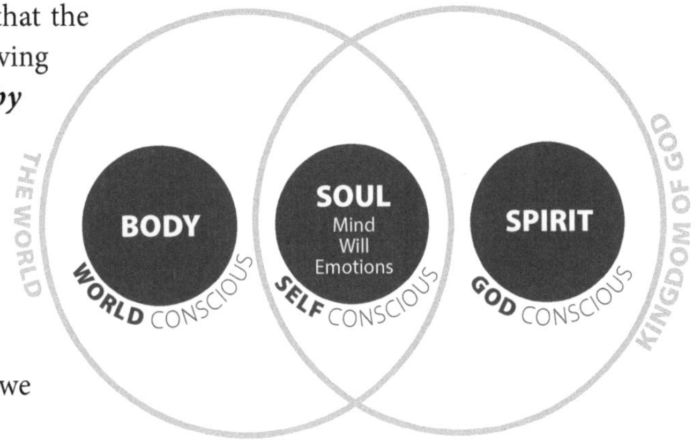

Our flesh and bones were created from the earth, so we

can relate to the earth—and everything in it. They relate through our five senses: sight, hearing, touch, taste and smell.

Now, although you might think that our bodies are mere *earth suits* to carry our spirit and soul, they're actually ***fearfully and wonderfully made*** (***Psalm 139:14***) and something that we must look after. ***1 Corinthians 6:19-20 (NLT)*** asks, ***"Don't you realize that your body is the temple of the Holy Spirit, who lives in you and was given to you by God? You do not belong to yourself, for God bought you with a high price. So you must honor God with your body."*** We have to feed it properly, water it repeatedly, rest it well and exercise it regularly.

Having said that, it's ultimately important that you get to know more of who you are in the spirit than who you are in the body.

QUESTIONS TO PONDER

- **How would you explain the difference between your soul and your spirit? Why is the difference important?**
- **What five benefits could you name of having God himself living inside you? How can you maximise these in your life?**
- **God is a spirit and so are you. How does that make you feel about the 'physical' you?**
- **As your body is a temple of God, how are you looking after it? What one thing can you implement today that will help you do better with that? And how will you ensure you stay on track?**

YESTERDAY'S SUMMARY: You are spirit, you have a soul and you live in a body. When you were born again, your spirit was infused with the life of Christ and you now are known in heaven by his righteousness.

DAY 3

THE TWO NATURES

FOLLOWING ON FROM yesterday's teaching, today we will dive a little deeper and learn about the battle that so often rages in us as Christians.

Every believer experiences the truth and reality of their dual nature, but not all can explain what is going on inside them. So let's give that a go.

Every person is born with just one nature that is inherited from Adam. You might have heard this referred to as the *sin* or *sinful* nature. This description implies that Christians still have an intrinsic malfunction in their *new creation* (**2 Corinthians 5:17**) where old things, not least our relationship with sin, have actually been radically changed. In old language this nature is called *the flesh* (which is harder to explain, but probably more accurate).

Both terms in the right context are interchangeable and we'll use them throughout this book. You may also see more general terms like *carnal nature* or *old nature* being used. They're all one and the same thing.

Whichever title we give it, we need to know what it's like. In a nutshell, it's a nature that deceives us into thinking and acting in worldly ('fleshly') ways that don't represent God's agenda for mankind in any way, shape or form. ***1 Corinthians 2:14 (ESV)*** tells us that ***"The natural person does not accept the things of the Spirit of God, for they are folly to him, and he is not able to understand them because they are spiritually discerned."***

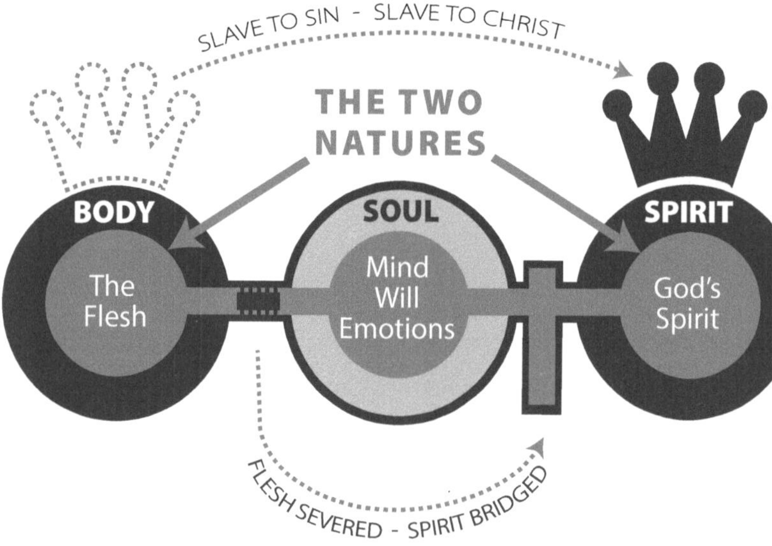

Another way of looking at the two natures is in terms of *capacities*. The old nature has the capacity to sin; the new nature has the capacity to resist sin—and, just as important, the desire to live in a godly way. ***Romans 6:6 (NLT)*** explains that ***"our old sinful selves were crucified with Christ so that sin might lose its power in our lives. We are no longer slaves to sin."*** A few lines on verse 18 exclaims, ***"now you are free from your slavery to sin, and you have become slaves to righteous living."***

At the point of finding new life in Christ—being born again—you received a completely new nature. The old nature came by natural birth (through Adam), but the new nature came by spiritual birth (through Jesus—also referred to as *the last Adam*). But it's not a *replacement* nature; rather, an *additional* one. Unfortunately, whilst we are in our human bodies, we will always have the old nature to contend with to some degree. In Week Three we'll *flesh* this out a lot more—see what I did there?

This is the conflict every Christian carries inside them. Even the great Apostle Paul explains his battle with his old nature in ***Romans 7:22-23 (AMP),*** speaking of the inner turmoil going on: ***"For I joyfully delight in the law of God in my inner self [with my new nature], but I see a different law and rule of action in the members of my body [in its appetites and desires], waging war against the law of my mind and subduing me and making me a prisoner of the law of sin which is within my members."***

A vitally important aspect of these natures to grasp is this: they are in opposition to one another. ***Galatians 5:17 (NLT)*** encapsulates this by declaring, ***"The sinful nature wants to do evil, which is just the opposite of what the Spirit wants. And the Spirit gives us desires that are the opposite of what the sinful nature desires. These two forces are constantly fighting each other, so you are not free to carry out your good intentions."*** Then in verses 19-21 it says, ***"When you follow the desires of your sinful nature, the results are very clear: sexual immorality, impurity, lustful pleasures, idolatry, sorcery, hostility, quarreling, jealousy, outbursts of anger, selfish ambition, dissension, division, envy, drunkenness."*** And then in verses 22-23 the opposite nature is exposed: ***"But the Holy Spirit produces this kind of fruit in our lives: love, joy, peace, patience, kindness, goodness, faithfulness, gentleness, and self-control. There is no law against these things!"***

Even though your new nature is fully good—being influenced by the Holy Spirit living inside you—your old nature is fully bad, drawing its influences from the godless world and evil spirits around you. It opposes everything God desires. This tension often results in many Christians experiencing a continual seesawing of emotions and behaviours that can one minute bring glory to God, and the next condemnation to self.

The two natures wage war inside you and every other born-again person on the planet. If you've never experienced this, then the chances are that you've never really been saved!

And it's important to understand that the battle starts and finishes in the mind. This is the battleground for every believer, so we should put a lot of energy and focus on guarding our minds from evil thoughts that come our way.

The enemy also tries to take us down by leading us into places and situations where we automatically think fleshly thoughts. Wherever we are, we should get into the practice of testing every thought before it can lead to action. ***2 Corinthians 10:5 (NIVUK)*** tells us to, ***"take captive every thought to make it obedient to Christ."*** Train yourself to do this and you'll save yourself a lot of problems that the devil is trying to give you!

QUESTIONS TO PONDER

- **In what ways have you chosen to walk according to your fleshly nature recently? How can you prevent that from happening again?**
- **How do you feel when you choose your old nature instead of the Spirit?**
- **In what ways have you chosen to walk in the Spirit today? What were the consequences?**
- **If you had to describe what being 'a slave to Christ' means, what three things would you say?**

YESTERDAY'S SUMMARY: At salvation your spirit became alive and connected to your soul; the power of your old nature got severed and you no longer have to live the way you used to do, in rebellion to God.

DAY 4

IN HIM

LET'S LOOK TODAY at us being in him. By *him* I mean Christ. But also I mean God. And when I talk about us being in him (Christ and/or God), it's as much about Christ (and/or God) being in *us*, as it is us being in either (or both) of them!

Did you follow that? Probably not! Let's try again...

You may have been taught that ***Luke 11*** and ***Matthew 6*** contain the Lord's Prayer. Well, technically that's not true, because in those passages the Lord *teaches* on prayer. The actual *Lord's* prayer is found in John chapter 17. In this narrative, Jesus starts by praying for himself, then he goes on to pray for his disciples, and he ends by praying for you and me as part of all future believers. Let's pull out a few verses...

We'll start in ***John 17:10 (NIVUK)*** where Jesus prayed to his Father, ***"All I have is yours, and all you have is mine. And glory has come to me***

through them." Think of the glory that Jesus received from the Father. This is the same glory Moses wanted to see, and although God granted his request in that he passed by him, he had to prevent Moses from seeing his face. Such was the radiance of God's glory that one glimpse of it would have killed him! King David wrote in ***Psalm 19:1 (NIVUK), "The heavens declare the glory of God; the skies proclaim the work of his hands."*** God's glory is vast and powerful.

Listen to this: That same glory is in you! ***John 17:22 (NIVUK)*** says, ***"I have given them the glory that you gave me."*** Take a moment to let that sink in. God shared his glory with Jesus, and in turn Jesus shares that same glory with us, so to be born again means that you have Christ glorified in you.

It doesn't matter whether you feel like you're the worst Christian in the world; it doesn't matter if you're struggling with habitual sin; it doesn't matter if you're struggling to forgive. All these are sins that you should deal with, but they're not recorded in your copy book because Christ dealt with the penalty of all your shortcomings 2000 years ago on the cross.

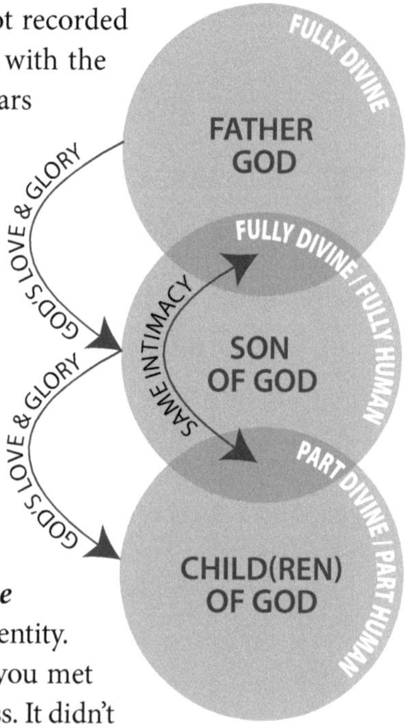

God's glory is in you—not because of anything you've done, but because of everything Jesus has done. You can be at the lowest point in your Christian life, but that's when you need to experience his glory the most!

2 Corinthians 4:6 (NIVUK) says, ***"For God, who said, 'Let light shine out of darkness,' made his light shine in our hearts to give us the light of the knowledge of God's glory displayed in the face of Christ."*** Darkness is not in itself an entity. Darkness is the absence of light. Before you met Christ you were in the kingdom of darkness. It didn't matter how much of a *good person* you may have been; when it came to the things of the Spirit it was pitch black. But when you met Jesus and accepted him into your life, the light of the world got switched on inside you like a stadium floodlight buzzing with power. He is blazing in your spirit right now.

You can't turn the power down, but you can dim the effect of his glory with sin. Even on the most dismal, dark, dank day, the sun is shining as brightly as ever; it just has clouds in the way of it. So it is with our sin. It prevents us from basking in the glory; it dulls our fellowship with God. But let's make it clear: our spiritual position is one of glory. Christ's glory still burns brightly inside us. This is the true hope to which we were called. ***Colossians 1:27 (NKJV)*** puts it, ***"To them God willed to make known what are the riches of the glory of this mystery among the Gentiles: which is Christ in you, the hope of glory."***

Back to Jesus' prayer. A few verses further on, in ***John 17:26 (NIVUK),*** he prays to his Father, ***"I have made you known to them, and will continue to make you known in order that the love you have for me may be in them and that I myself may be in them."*** Just as God's glory has been passed down to us through Christ, so too is his love.

We can know the natural love a father has for his child. You may have firsthand experience of this. Take all the potential human failures away from both parties; now imagine that wonderful, loving relationship in action. What you're seeing is just a finite glimpse of how much Father God infinitely and perfectly loves his Son. Here's the mic drop moment: God loves you with that same love! The truth is you can't do anything bad (or fail to do anything good) that will take away even the smallest part of his love for you.

Luke 15 gives us the wonderful account of the Prodigal Son. I'd encourage you to read it right after you've finished this chapter. It shows how we're never too far away from the love of God, and that there's no line of unforgiveness we can knowingly step over. This sentiment is echoed in ***Romans 5:8 (AMP): "God clearly shows and proves His own love for us, by the fact that while we were still sinners, Christ died for us."*** And also, in the often quoted ***John 3:16 (NIVUK), "For God so loved the world that he gave his one and only Son, that whoever believes in him shall not perish but have eternal life."*** God is crazy in love with you. If he had a phone, he'd have a photo of you on his lock screen.

And if the sharing of God's love and glory weren't enough to grasp, we are also told that the same access Jesus had with the Father, we have too!

Most people in the world cry out to God only in times of desperation. Even though they are spiritually dead, there's still something in their soul that instinctively calls out to him. But those of us who are born again, who have come alive spiritually, have full access to God. You can experience his love and forgiveness any time you choose. There's no waiting in line. You can come into his glorious presence boldly, confident that he is both wanting and waiting to talk with you. You can open your heart to him and, through confession, have every cloud of sin blown away. What's stopping you doing that right now?

QUESTIONS TO PONDER

- **Have you ever considered that God wants the same relationship with you as he did with Jesus on the earth? How different might that look to what it's like now?**
- **How does it make you feel that when God looks at your spirit he sees Jesus?**
- **Do you find it hard to accept that you're made in God's image, and that God's glory blazes inside you? If so, why do you think that? And how can you align yourself more with the truth?**
- **What sins are currently clouding the glory of God in your life right now? What would it take to confess them?**

YESTERDAY'S SUMMARY: Because Christ was sacrificed, God's love for him is now also in you. So too is his wonderful glory blazing in your heart. When God looks at your spirit, it's like he's looking at Jesus!

DAY 5 — ANOTHER DIMENSION

THE TITLE 'SAINT' seems a lofty one for us to own, but as we've been finding out it's fully justified and apt—all because Christ now lives in us and we've taken on his righteousness.

It's totally acceptable for Christians to be addressed as saints—just as the Apostle Paul did to the churches he wrote to—but you won't find your unsaved neighbour or boss addressing you with that title! Without sounding patronising, they don't get it. And can't get it. ***1 Corinthians 2:14 (NIVUK)*** tells us that, ***"The person without the Spirit does not accept the things that come from the Spirit of God but considers them foolishness, and cannot understand them because they are discerned only through the Spirit."*** It's a spiritual thing. We're spiritual people—with a soul, living in a body.

But there appears to be a problem. Not just the devil. Not just our flesh. The problem is the world. We've always been familiar with our natural surroundings and homelands, but in Christ we transferred our place of residence from earth to heaven. According to the legal authorities of this world, my passport says I'm British; but God, the eternal judge of the universe, says I'm a newborn citizen of heaven. ***Philippians 3:19-20 (NIVUK)***, talking of people of the world, says that ***"Their mind is set on earthly things. But our citizenship is in heaven."***

So we're from the perfect place of heaven—great! But we live in a sin-infested world—not so great. The contrast is stark. And it's not just a metaphorical one; we live with the actual tensions of it every day. The old, familiar ways of the world are still etched in our souls. We see their inner workings everywhere we go, but we aren't to follow them any more. As ***Romans 12:2 (NLT)*** says, ***"Don't copy the behavior and customs of this world, but let God transform you into a new person by changing the way you think."***

Okay, we're spiritual beings, but this body we live in is firmly rooted on planet earth. That's how it was meant to be right from the beginning. Our incredibly designed and functioning body has its senses—sight, sound, touch, smell and taste—all intrinsically linked to this world. We breathe in oxygen that comes from the earth's trees and plants, and the water we need to survive comes from the skies. It's all the outworking of God's master plan that we read in the creation account.

The tension between these two worlds is plain to see. It may seem like we just have to hold out for heaven, but that's not the case. Why? Because heaven is already here! "But I thought we go to heaven when we die," you may be thinking. We do. But we have to understand *what* heaven is, not just *where* it is!

Let's just quickly cover the *where,* because we don't really know that. All that's inferred is that it's *upward,* so that's all we need to know.

Regarding the nature of heaven, we need to first recognise that it's a real, but spiritual, dimension. At the end of time a physical heaven is depicted as coming down onto a new earth. It's all recorded in the Apostle

John's vision in ***Revelation 21:1-4 (NIVUK). "Then I saw 'a new heaven and a new earth,' for the first heaven and the first earth had passed away, and there was no longer any sea. I saw the Holy City, the new Jerusalem, coming down out of heaven from God, prepared as a bride beautifully dressed for her husband. And I heard a loud voice from the throne saying, 'Look! God's dwelling-place is now among the people, and he will dwell with them. They will be his people, and God himself will be with them and be their God. "He will wipe every tear from their eyes. There will be no more death" or mourning or crying or pain, for the old order of things has passed away.'"***

Christians often think that heaven will be some immaterial, floaty place in the sky, but it seems that couldn't be further from the truth. A heavenly 'city' will be our eternal resting place on a new physical earth. How it all pans out in reality we don't know, but we do know that the global Church will live there—both serving and worshipping God. As believers we aren't going to be judged for our sins, but the unbelievers are; the penalty for our sins was dealt with 2000 years ago. We're still going to face Christ's judgment, but he's going to assess our life and service in him and as a result we'll receive various rewards that we will take into our eternal dwelling.

With that all said, this physical world we currently live in shouldn't be seen as irrelevant, because it's the realm we were designed to live in from the very beginning and—in its newness, void of sin— it's the realm that we'll be reunited with in the end.

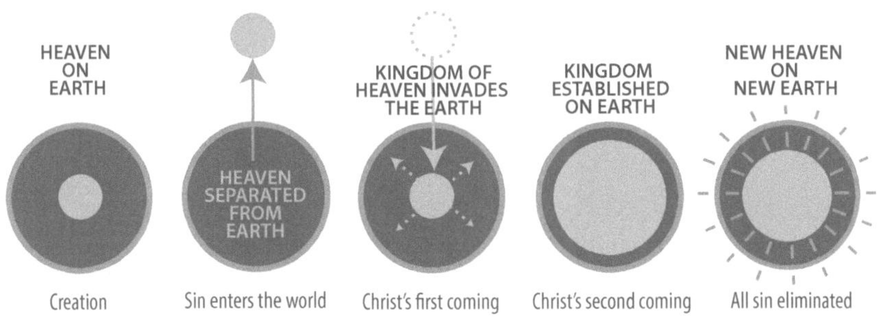

But we don't have to wait for that physical reality to emerge, because we have the spiritual dimension available to us right now: the *Kingdom* of Heaven. Jesus announced in ***Matthew 4:17 (NKJV)*** that ***"the kingdom of God is at hand"***. It's coming, but it's also here—just as our ultimate salvation is coming when Christ returns, but we're experiencing it in the here and now. And when Jesus comes back a second time he will fully establish his Kingdom on earth for a thousand years. After that, eternity will kick in with the new heaven and new earth. (I'm acutely aware that not everyone will hold this precise view of end-time events. If that's you, just make sure that you don't let that cloud the main point I'm making.)

We shouldn't shy away from this world; we should engage in it. As ambassadors of the Kingdom we should be representing it well by exhibiting heaven's culture and invading our world with the Kingdom message of salvation. Although there's been an invasion of sin in the world, this is still God's created earth and we are God's created people. Together we have a mandate to make a difference in people's lives.

QUESTIONS TO PONDER

- **Is the Kingdom of heaven a significant reality in your life? How could it be more?**
- **How good an ambassador for the Kingdom of God do you think you are in this world? What do you think are some of the key responsibilities for such a position?**
- **What does it mean to you to be '*in* the world, but not *of* it'?**
- **How does the revealed big picture of God's eternal plan affect how you live as a Christian in the here and now?**

YESTERDAY'S SUMMARY: We are no longer 'of' the world, but we are in it and should engage with it appropriately.

DAY 6

SAVIOUR & LORD

JESUS IS SO many things to us: he's our lover, our friend, our redeemer, our high priest, our king, our peace, our hope, our rock… we could go on for some time! But two attributes and titles that are headlined in the scriptures for born-again believers are Jesus is our 'Saviour' and 'Lord'.

Romans 10:9 (ESV) says, ***"if you confess with your mouth that Jesus is Lord and believe in your heart that God raised him from the dead, you will be saved"*** (emphasis mine).

It's reasonable to estimate that Jesus is Saviour to between one and two billion people across the globe. God has revealed himself to them through the work and words of his Son, Jesus Christ. By faith they have supernaturally believed in his life, death and resurrection, declaring that Jesus is Lord of all—not least of their own lives.

But within months, maybe even weeks, that newfound intimacy with God can start to wane. We can start to lose our joy; we might not be as 'on fire' for the things of God as we used to be; we might start to lose our temper too quickly and too often; we may encounter more frustrations than normal. It's called backsliding. We don't always see it as that because we still love Jesus, we still believe, we still go to church, we're even still reading our Bibles. But these things have nothing to do with living out our lives under the lordship of Christ, and our submission to him.

Yes, of course there is a part of the 'new' in any relationship that has a shelf-life, but the new life in Christ lasts forever. Now, please let what I'm about to say sink in; take a moment to read slowly and digest it. The intimacy experienced with God at salvation—and in the following weeks, months and years—is not meant to dissipate. It's meant to grow. It grieves God when we are not as close as we once were; when we start flirting with the world it affects him. He's a jealous God (***Exodus 34:14***). His heart's desire is to pour out his unending love for us; to show us great and wonderful things, and increase our quality time together.

So why does the 'honeymoon period' end? It ends because we first confess him as Lord of our lives, but then gradually start taking back lordship ourselves.

Your enemy the devil knows that your salvation can't be taken from you, but he *can* get you to relinquish the lordship of Jesus Christ that you confessed at salvation. If he can get you to take back control of your life, then he can make your salvation experience as miserable, as frustrating and as ineffective as possible. You can be happy about being saved, but that doesn't mean you'll be full of joy. There's a joy of the Lord ***(Nehemiah 8:10)***, as well as a joy of salvation ***(Psalm 51:12)***.

When Jesus returns it's going to be a leveller for all mankind. The whole world is going to recognise him as Lord—including you and me. ***Philippians 2:9-11 (AMP)*** tells us that ***"God has highly exalted Him and bestowed on Him the name which is above every name, so that at the name of Jesus every knee shall bow [in submission], of those who are in***

heaven and on earth and under the earth, and that every tongue will confess and openly acknowledge that Jesus Christ is Lord (sovereign God), to the glory of God the Father." In light of this physical revelation of his majesty, many Christians will see the lack of lordship that has taken place in their lives.

In heaven there won't be any capacity to sin. We won't know what it is to take our own lordship but we will live totally submitted to his will, doing as he pleases. If that's what's going to happen forever, then we may as well get some practice in now!

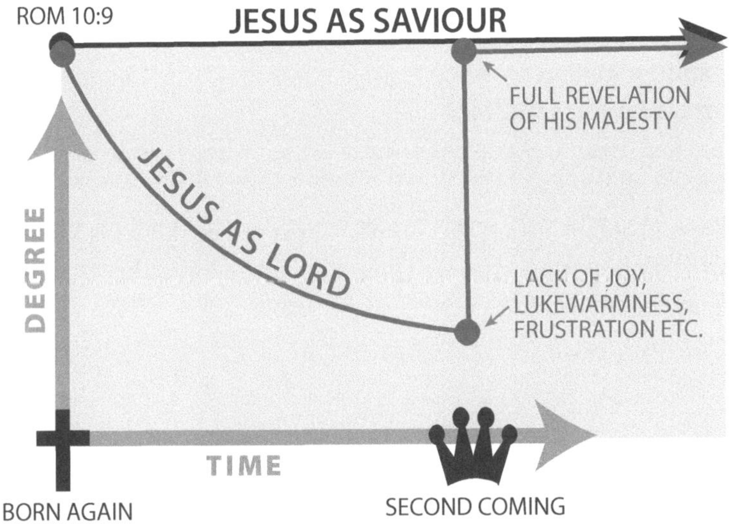

Proverbs 3:5-6 (NIVUK) says, ***"Trust in the Lord with all your heart and lean not on your own understanding; in all your ways submit to him, and he will make your paths straight."*** There's a path of life that we all take as Christians. Unfortunately, whilst living in this sin-infested world we get taken off course so easily (as illustrated above). But to keep us on the straight and narrow path, God gives us the formula: trust Jesus wholeheartedly, rather than yourself; live under his lordship and the path of life will be clear to see. The chartered course of a Christian is not always easy, but we can keep pressing on when Jesus is at the helm and

we're living every moment of every day in submission to him, fully trusting in him rather than ourselves.

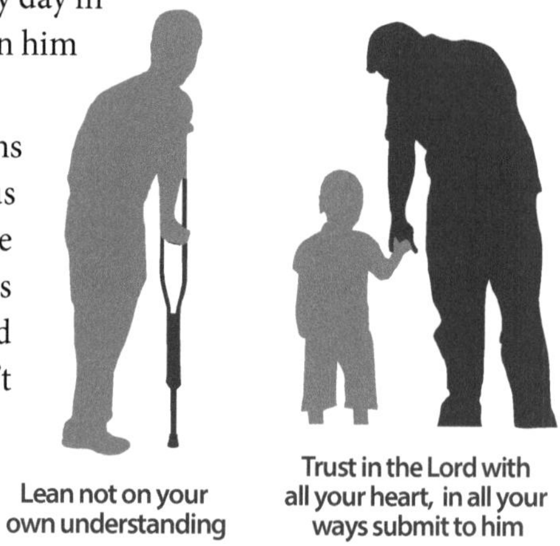

People often say that Christians are weak because they need Jesus as a crutch, but a better and more accurate picture of a Christian is that of a small child walking hand in hand with their father. God isn't our crutch; he's given us two feet to stand on, but we can take his hand and be guided by him. Why would I want to take back lordship and trust my vulnerable, imperfect self when I can trust the One who knows all things?

Every kingdom has a king. One day Christ will establish his Kingdom on earth. It's important that we come to realise now, rather than later, that *Jesus* is Lord—not us.

QUESTIONS TO PONDER

- **Looking back on your Christian life, do you recall being more on fire for God than you are now? If you do, what was different in your walk with God then?**
- **If you're going to be fully committed to serving Jesus as Lord throughout all eternity, what's stopping you being fully committed now?**
- **Do you think it's possible to trust God with all your heart, and submit every last way to him? If so, what would that look like for you in practice?**

YESTERDAY'S SUMMARY: Accepting Jesus as Lord gets you into heaven, but making Jesus Lord determines how you get there—as well as how things pan out when you're there!

DAY 7
LOVE & FEAR

WHEN I WAS around seven years of age, I went out to play with my older brother and our next door neighbour one Sunday afternoon. It was the late '70s, when a playstation was a swing and a slide in the back garden.

On that particular day we decided to go and explore the empty fields at the bottom of our road. Along one edge was a stream with a row of fenced-off factories running parallel to it. That day as we walked by the stream we came to a breach in the wire fence. Part of it had come away, and without much strain we were able to open it up even further and slip through into the back of a huge crane factory. It suddenly felt like we were in all the suspense of a Bond movie.

Thinking that no one would be there on a weekend, the yard became a vast, exciting new adventure land. That was until a foreman spotted us and apprehended us with a deep, bellowing shout. It was now a fight-or-flight moment. My brother ran; my neighbour and I froze.

We were caught in the act of trespassing. We weren't 'bad' kids; we were raised well, so this was unknown territory for us.

After a short, reprimanding discourse from the seemingly frightful crane factory worker, he said the words that none of us wanted to hear: "Do you want me to *tell your fathers* what you've been up to?" I remember it like yesterday. A whole new level of fear suddenly got mixed in with the adrenaline already pumping through our veins. If you were born in the '80s, '90s or '00s, you might struggle to equate what I'm saying. But anyone born in the '70s or earlier will understand, because back then kids were taught to have respect for their parents—especially their dad as the *head of the home*. Sadly, that's nowhere near as prominent as it used to be (and where it's prominent, it's unfortunately often abused.)

The church majors heavily on the love of God. I'm sure you can reel off some classic *love* scriptures, right? I hope so. Any of which I'm sure would be truly great and helpful in our understanding of God. But there are plenty of verses about *fearing the Lord,* too. Do you have any of *them* memorised?

In order to have a greater intimacy with God, we're going to need a greater understanding of who he is. We need to know that as well as personifying love (***1 John 4:8***), God is also a consuming fire (***Hebrews 12:29***)! As well as being gentle and humble (***Matthew 11:29***) he is fierce and powerful (***Exodus 15:6***). God isn't schizophrenic; he just has more to him than we think. These two aspects of his nature could be viewed as two sides of the same coin. It's imperative that we have both a loving and a reverential relationship with God.

Before we continue further on this thought, let's make absolutely sure that we're clear on this: the fear of the Lord has nothing to do with the spirit of fear! ***1 John 4:18 (NIVUK)*** tells us that ***"There is no fear in love. But perfect love drives out fear."***

Exodus 20:18-20 (NIVUK) highlights the difference between the two. God has just miraculously delivered his people from the land of slavery in Egypt and now has them at the foot of Mount Sinai, where he gives them his standard for living: the Ten Commandments. When the people saw the smoke, thunder and lightning, and heard the trumpet blast, they trembled with fear. Staying at a distance they said to Moses, ***"Speak to us yourself and we will listen. But do not have God speak to us or we will die." Moses said to the people, "Do not be afraid. God has come to test you, so that the fear of God will be with you to keep you from sinning"*** (emphasis mine). The difference here is that Moses had the *fear of the Lord* whilst the people were *afraid of God.*

God is not a God in the sky who wants to beat us with a stick. He's an almighty, all-loving God for whom we should have the greatest respect as we feel the warmth of his embrace. The more we see God in his majesty, the more in awe of him we become.

And this is not just an Old Testament phenomenon; throughout scripture we are told to 'fear' God. For instance, Peter bluntly instructs us in ***1 Peter 2:17 (NIVUK)*** to ***"fear God".*** Paul and the church at Corinth knew what it was to fear the Lord. ***2 Corinthians 5:11 (NLT)*** tells us, ***"Because we understand our fearful responsibility to the Lord, we work hard to persuade others."*** And even Jesus instructed his disciples, ***"fear the One who, after He has killed, has authority and power to hurl [you] into hell; yes, I say to you, [stand in great awe of God and] fear Him!" (Luke 12:5, AMP).***

If we have both the love of God *and* the fear of God in our hearts, then we can be truly intimate with him. Imagine loving someone for years and later finding out that there was a significant part of their good nature that you were unaware of. You wouldn't have been able to appreciate them as much as you could have done. That can be the same with us and God. When we understand God's holiness we can be in greater awe of him. There will be more of him for us to draw close to. Not only will we have more of him to love, but it means that we can approach him in a more respectful way, too.

Psalm 25:14 (NLT) confirms to us that, ***"The Lord is a friend to those who fear him. He teaches them his covenant."***

QUESTIONS TO PONDER

- **How do you think the world would look if God was all love with no holiness? What about the other way around?**
- **Would you say you have a healthy quota of both the love of God and the fear of God in your life?**
- **Has the behaviour of a natural father hindered your relationship with God the Father? How has the enemy used this ? What one step could you implement to start putting God back in his rightful place?**
- **In what ways do you exhibit the fear of God in your life? If you can't think of any, what can you do about that?**

WEEK 1 SUMMARY

Day 1: Knowing God – Eternal life is to know God intimately from the moment of being born again, not just waiting for the afterlife.

Day 2: Three-part Beings – You are spirit, you have a soul and you live in a body. When you were born again, your spirit was infused with the life of Christ and now you are known in heaven by his righteousness.

Day 3: The Two Natures – At salvation, your spirit became alive and connected to your soul; the power of your old nature got severed and you no longer have to live the way you used to do, in rebellion to God.

Day 4: In Him – Because Christ was sacrificed, God's love for him is now also in you. So too is his wonderful glory blazing in your heart. When God looks at your spirit, it's like he's looking at Jesus!

Day 5: Another Dimension – We are no longer 'of' the world, but we are in it and should engage with it appropriately.

Day 6: Saviour & Lord – Accepting Jesus as Lord gets you into heaven, but making Jesus Lord determines how you get there—as well as how things pan out when you're there!

Day 7: Love & Fear – Having a healthy reverence towards God is as important as showing your love for him.

The pursuit of mankind
isn't happiness
but holiness.

WEEK 2

The journey into intimacy: SANCTIFICATION

FROM JUSTIFICATION TO SANCTIFICATION

So last week we looked at themes surrounding our position in Christ. The moment we were born again everything changed: we became new creations; the power of the flesh was cut off; the Spirit of God made us spiritually alive; we were sinners, we became saints; God came to live in us by his Holy Spirit. It's all connected to the word *Justification*.

The next weird-sounding word that we'll be using as a common point of reference this week is *Sanctification*. If justification is what happened when we were saved, then sanctification is the intended maturity in Christ that happens to us from that point on until Jesus returns. It all takes place during our 'being saved' experience.

Put simply, sanctification is the increasing disconnect from sin in our lives, making us more and more like Jesus.

Being saved is necessary to obtain eternal life in the new heaven on our new earth, but being sanctified is how we make the most of that eternal life in God whilst we're on *this* earth!

Your salvation is God's gift to you; your sanctification is your gift to God.

CHRIST-LIKENESS

Just as any decent father wants his children to turn out well, so too Father God wants his children to flourish. Our performance doesn't affect our position in Christ, but it does affect how we bring glory and honour to him.

Sanctification is about becoming Christ-like, but we can only become like him when we're in him. They say that you become like the three people you hang around with most. I think that's true to a large degree, and it's certainly true when it comes to the Father, the Son and the Holy Spirit. The more time we spend in God's presence, the more we acknowledge him in everything, the more familiar we become with his ways, the more he will 'rub off' on us.

We have a *union* with Christ when we're saved—that is fixed; we have a *communion* as we follow Christ—that ebbs and flows. The idea is that we increase the inward flows and decrease the outward ebbs. The end goal of sanctification is complete holiness at the point Christ returns for his Church; until then we can go on the world's greatest adventure as we build up our relationship with God.

He desires to work through us, whether that's with love, grace, miracles, compassion, or whatever else that has the goodness of God written all over it. He wants to relate to us just as he related to Jesus in his life on earth.

He has special works for us to do; he has holy assignments with our name on them. We are his hands and feet in this world and he has much to accomplish through us.

NEXT LEVEL

The truth is there are always new levels of growth that Christ has for us. The problem, however, is this: our tendency is to settle for the status quo, stick with the familiar and keep to our spiritual routines that are working very well for us, thank you very much. But the point is that there's always more.

Philippians 4:13 (AMP) says, ***"I can do all things [which He has called me to do] through Him who strengthens and empowers me [to fulfill His purpose—I am self-sufficient in Christ's sufficiency; I am ready for anything and equal to anything through Him who infuses me with inner strength and confident peace.]"***

God has given us everything we need in Christ Jesus—we just need to use it. The same power that is in Christ Jesus is living in us—we just need to release it. We've been blessed with every spiritual blessing in the heavenly realms—we just need it to flow out of us. These provisions, blessings and powers manifest themselves in different ways with different people, but they're all locked up inside every believer—including you! We see them in action as we grow in God, as we spend more time in his presence, as we go to new levels of belief, and as we endure like we've never endured and trust like we've never trusted. The Father is training us as his children. Yes, there's often loving discipline, but we only grow when we spend time being taught, loved and encouraged by him.

RUNNING THE RACE

When our sanctification is complete at Christ's return we're going to be revealed as victors. We're going to win the race marked out for us. We're going to be on the side of the Conqueror.

I don't know about you, but I don't want to be limping into victory; I want to be running. I want to burst through the finish line full of life and resurrection energy. I know it's not going to be a walk in the park (not wanting to mix my metaphors up too much), that it will take discipline and there will be some unwanted surprises on the way, but my inner desire is to be the best version of me there can be, to go all in with God and to make him proud.

Remember, you died to the old, draining, fleshly nature that produced only selfish gain; you came alive to the new power-giving Spirit that produces righteousness. ***2 Timothy 1:7 (NLT)*** says, ***"For God has not given us a spirit of fear and timidity, but of power, love, and self-discipline."*** It's not normal any more for you to walk the trodden paths of this world, but it's perfectly normal for you to be one with God, to hear his voice regularly and to enjoy constant fellowship with him through the Holy Spirit.

So what do you say? Are you ready to taste once again of the goodness of God? Are you ready to take a fresh look at what's possible for you in the spiritual realm? Are you ready to explore the blessings that accompany intimacy with him? If so, let's go...

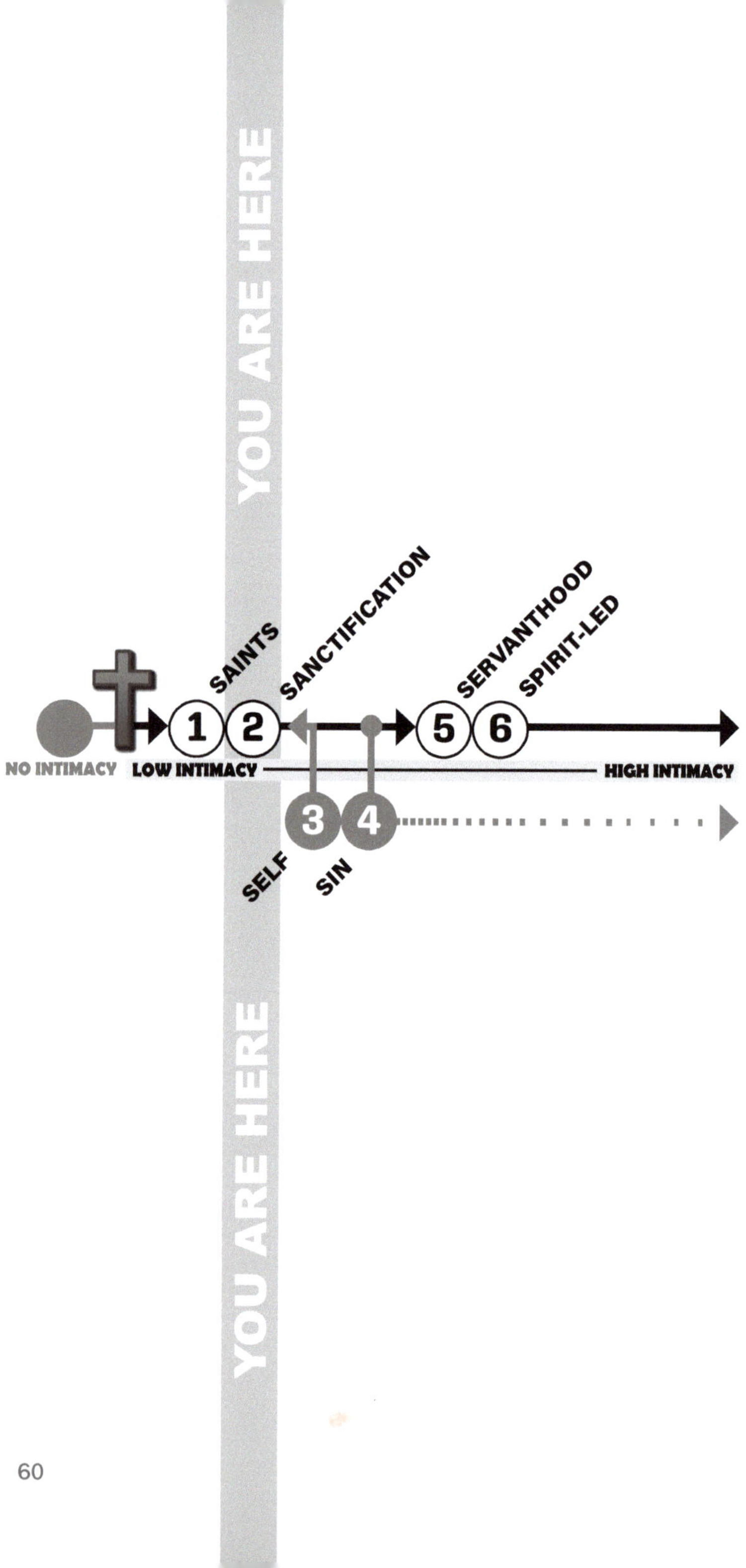
YOU ARE HERE
SAINTS
SANCTIFICATION
SERVANTHOOD
SPIRIT-LED
1
2
5
6
NO INTIMACY
LOW INTIMACY
HIGH INTIMACY
3
4
SELF
SIN
YOU ARE HERE

DAY 8

THRIVING OR SURVIVING?

I'D GUESS THAT a large percentage of Christians live a mediocre life when it comes to things of the Spirit. They're spiritually saved, but they're naturally stuck.

In the book of Exodus, we see God's people (called *Israel*) escaping from slavery in Egypt. Unfortunately, rather than taking a relatively short coastal trip to the Promised Land of Canaan, the nation of about two to three million ended up wandering round the wilderness for 40 years because they were a disobedient, complaining people. As a result, a whole generation didn't reach their ultimate destination.

It's been said that God got Israel out of Egypt, but he couldn't get Egypt out of Israel. We can find ourselves in a similar situation. We have a wonderful experience of God delivering us from the slavery of sin, but we so easily fall back into our old ways of living. We're happy to have him as *Saviour* in our Egypt, but being *Lord* in our wilderness is a different matter.

Egypt was a land of slavery and bondage for Israel. They were still God's people when they escaped into the wilderness, but they were only just surviving there. Satan wants you stuck wandering round the wilderness. You're still saved, God still loves you, but if he can keep you in a place of restriction then not only does he limit your effectiveness as a Christian, but he can limit (and even damage) your witness to non-Christians.

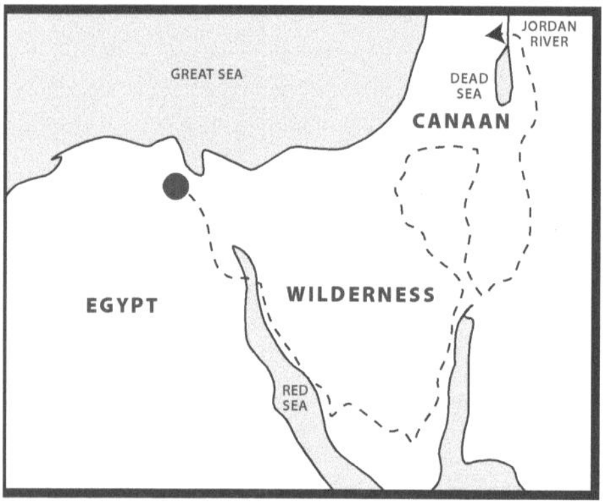

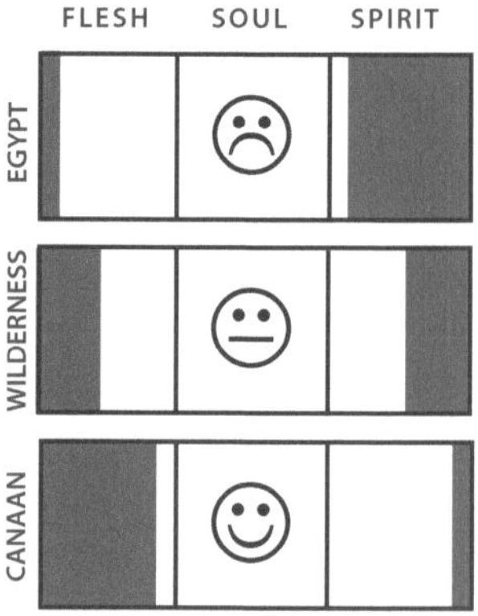

Irrespective of what's happening in our physical world, God wants us all to thrive spiritually within the Promised Land! Jesus said it like this in ***John 10:10 (AMP), "I came that they may have and enjoy life, and have it in abundance [to the full, till it overflows]."***

Thriving doesn't mean everything is going well without any challenges in life. You can be broke but thriving spiritually; you can be in grief but still experience the joy of the Lord; you can even be dying, but alive in Christ—***2 Corinthians 4:16 (NLT)*** states, ***"Though our bodies are dying, our spirits are being renewed every day."***

Our two natures are paramount in determining whether we are thriving in Canaan or surviving in the wilderness. If we walk according to what our old, carnal nature desires, we will reap the fruit of that nature (***Galatians 5:19-21***).

As Christians we either choose to be dictated to by the old flesh nature which brings about depression, frustration and anxiety, or by the new Spirit nature which exhibits a life of joy, hope and faith.

We can so easily put on our Sunday best and look like we've got it all together. I'm sure many of us have been all smiles during a church service, but at the same time masking resentment from an argument during the car journey in! Yes, we're all human; yes, we can all fall into sin so easily, but we don't have to live that way when we choose to obey our spirit rather than our flesh.

Whereas some Christians *look* like they are thriving but aren't, some actually are! They're alive in God. They're living in victory. They're in close communion with Jesus. They may be going through some battles, but they're winning. It may be hard, but they're on top. The lifestyle they live is not put on, it's real. And it's not happened by accident; it's happened on purpose.

If you asked a fellow Christian who's going through a challenging time how they're doing, they might say, 'Okay under the circumstances'. But we're not called to be *under* the circumstances; we're called to be *over* them (***1 John 4:4***). You may think that's just semantics, but the Bible says in ***Proverbs 23:7 (NKJV)*** of a man that ***"as he thinks in his heart, so is he."*** Too many Christians face problems in earthly ways, but we are instructed to live by faith, not by sight (***2 Corinthians 5:7***).

I am fully qualified at living a 'just enough' Christian life. For 20 years, on and off, I lived with an incurable bowel disease called colitis. Fortunately for me I didn't experience pain with it as many others do, but in the extreme of episodes it would paralyse me geographically in that I couldn't afford not to be within running distance of a toilet!

I lived *under* the circumstances for years, until one day I'd had enough of my wilderness living. A degree of righteous anger bubbled up inside me and I was determined to live *above* my circumstances. I was led by God to search the scriptures and find as many verses as I could on healing. I crammed them all onto two sides of an A4 sheet of paper by listing them in columns, narrowing the page margins, and reducing the font size to 6pt. I committed to reading them all once in the morning and once at night. It was like a spiritual prescription. ***Proverbs 4:20-22 (NKJV)*** says, ***"give attention to my words; Incline your ear to my sayings. Do not let them depart from your eyes; Keep them in the midst of your heart; For they are life to those who find them, And health to all their flesh."*** Within a month I had no symptoms and, 15 years on, not one flare-up for my consultant to note.

In order to thrive we must have intimacy. When we live in a close relationship with the Lord, listening to his voice and obeying his instructions, then we are truly blessed and thrive in our being. But when we only wear the Christian badge, turn up to a church service when it's convenient, serve now and again out of duty and pray only in times of need, we're actually living a Christian life of survival. And that's the best case scenario! The worst is that we live with things like condemnation, disappointment and depression.

QUESTIONS TO PONDER

- **Where are you stuck in life? Where are you wandering around in circles, making little to no progress?**
- **On a scale of 1 (surviving) to 10 (thriving), what number are you at? Why is that?**
- **What single action could get you one number higher? What could prevent you from achieving that, and how might you counteract it?**
- **What would it feel like to constantly live in the promises of God?**

YESTERDAY'S SUMMARY: Egypt was a land of 'not enough', the wilderness was a land of 'just enough', but the Promised Land was a land of 'more than enough'. Jesus died so you could live in the Promised Land.

DAY 9

BORN ON PURPOSE

WHEN IT COMES to Christianity, we shouldn't be sucked into universal thinking like, 'It's just one of hundreds of other religions'. It's not. It's different. Very different.

To start with, it's the only religion that teaches that God came to us. Judaism teaches that you can atone for sin by changing your behaviour, praying and doing good deeds. Islam tells you that you can move towards paradise by performing the Five Pillars. Hinduism claims that if you store up enough good karma then you'll reunite with the creator god Brahma. Buddhism says that you can achieve a state of Nirvana by practising the Eightfold Path. They all require us to reach God through works. But only in Christianity does God do the redemptive work for us!

Romans 5:8 (NLT) says that, ***"God showed his great love for us by sending Christ to die for us while we were still sinners."*** Jesus died for us before we did a thing for him. God didn't wait for us to get things right before he sent his Son to die. In fact, God sent his Son because he knew we could never get things right by our own efforts. Nowhere near—a perfect God requires perfection in order to access his presence.

So this is good news (more like incredible news), because we now get to speak to God. And not just that; when we choose to walk by the Spirit we experience the truth of ***Acts 17:28 (AMP),*** which says, ***"in Him we live and move and exist [that is, in Him we actually have our being], as even some of your own poets have said, 'For we also are His children.'"***

But entry into the Kingdom of God is not the end goal. It's just the beginning. This is when *our* work starts! A chant we love to echo in our church is this: 'We were born on purpose, for a purpose.' ***Ephesians 2:10 (AMP)*** says, ***"we are His workmanship [His own master work, a work of art], created in Christ Jesus [reborn from above—spiritually transformed, renewed, ready to be used] for good works, which God prepared [for us] beforehand [taking paths which He set], so that we would walk in them [living the good life which He prearranged and made ready for us]."*** Just as Adam and Eve were originally given work to do in managing the earth and populating it, this plan for us to do good things for God's glory is fully back on the agenda through Jesus Christ. ***Philippians 2:12 (NLT)*** instructs us, ***"Work hard to show the results of your salvation."***

We are saved by grace to first be someone: a child of God. We are then empowered by that same grace to do something: good works. It's my experience that the 21st century Church focuses more on the *being* than the *doing*. I understand fully the sentiment that God created us as human *beings*, not human *doings*, but out of our *walk* with God should flow our *work* with God.

Here's the bottom line: you were saved by the works *of* God, to do works *with* God, and *for* God. And when our salvation is completed in terms of receiving our new, glorified bodies at the end of the age, that too is a work of Christ. (It's actually more of a fulfilment of the finished work that he completed on the cross, but the point is it's *his* work, not *ours.*)

As a pastor, I've experienced countless numbers of Christians who have acted like spectators in God's Kingdom. They've misunderstood the

	JUSTIFICATION	**SANCTIFICATION**	GLORIFICATION
WHERE	SPIRIT	**SOUL**	BODY
WHEN	PAST	**PRESENT**	FUTURE
WHO	CHRIST	**US**	CHRIST

significance of their calling and the importance of the work that God has pre-planned for them to do.

That importance is clearly shown in Jesus' parable of the landowner who returns from a business trip. There are actually two similar parables telling two different stories, but the common understanding in both is that Jesus is that master and we are the servants. Jesus is returning to give rewards that we're going to receive and benefit from for all eternity.

Think about that for a moment. Every command that Jesus gives us today will have a bearing for countless billions of years to come. With that in mind it should be of paramount importance to us all that we pursue intimacy with him and learn to hear his voice of instruction. Instead, we settle for guessing what he wants us to do, assuming or—at worst—being tricked into thinking it's something other than what he actually wants. But if *our* good works aren't *God's* good works, then they will eventually get burned up by fire, yielding no return. ***1 Corinthians 3:12-15 (NIVUK)*** pulls no punches when it declares, ***"If anyone builds on this foundation using gold, silver, costly stones, wood, hay or straw, their work will be shown for what it is, because the Day will bring it to light. It will be revealed with fire, and the fire will test the quality***

of each person's work. If what has been built survives, the builder will receive a reward. If it is burned up, the builder will suffer loss but yet will be saved—even though only as one escaping through the flames."

Our work is ongoing. It's every day. Sometimes it's a task or project; sometimes it's being obedient or just having faith. But whatever it is, it can't be completed to any significant degree without hearing the voice of our Master. Some Christians may see this as an impossibility, but Jesus is crystal clear when he says, ***"The sheep that are My own hear My voice and listen to Me; I know them, and they follow Me." (John 10:27, AMP).***

You might think that you can't hear God like other Christians; that's simply not true! And it contradicts scripture. The book of James tells us that the great prophet Elijah was a man ***"just like us"*** (***James 5:17***). After three and a half years of drought God told him to pray for rain, and it rained. So we can hear God direct us too. It might be an everyday simple instruction, or it might be a more significant task.

QUESTIONS TO PONDER

- **What everyday commands of the Bible could you be better at obeying?**
- **How might these affect your relationship with God if you delay or disobey them?**
- **When it comes to your big-picture calling in life, are you active or are you stuck? If the latter, what are you going to do about it? If you don't know what your calling is, how are you going to get help finding that out?**
- **How can you better hear the voice of God so you can get done any future assignment he has for you?**

YESTERDAY'S SUMMARY: We were saved by God's good works in order to do good works for him, which he prepared for us long ago.

DAY 10

RELIGION VS RELATIONSHIP

AS WE CONTINUE to focus on the theme of sanctification, let's look at the part God plays in our being born again.

We saw yesterday that Christianity is the only religion where our good works aren't necessary for salvation. This leads us into another major difference that sets believers in Christ apart from believers of any other acclaimed deity. That is: Christianity is a religion that's centred around a relationship. A relationship with God. A relationship with a *living* God. A personal, intimate relationship, where God's followers are submitted to him as Lord and Master, but also enjoy the benefits of being his children (***John 1:12***)—and, to some extent, even friends of God (***John 15:15***).

Most religions seek to find satisfaction in the soul, understanding that in some way we are incomplete and imperfect in this realm of life. They search to find that fulfilment in different works, but only in Christianity is that completeness found in the works of someone else. Only Christianity faces the reality that, with all our best intentions and endeavours, no one is good enough to attain the perfect life that would be required to relate to a perfect God.

At the end of the creation account in Genesis chapter one, God unveiled his greatest masterpiece: man. This was not just any human, but a being made in God's own image. One designed to talk and walk with him (***Genesis 3:8***). Unfortunately it only took until chapter two to read about the severing of mankind's intimate relationship with God because of Adam's disobedience in the garden.

Fast-forward some 4000 years later and we see a rescue plan initiated and completed through the person of Jesus Christ—God's one and only Son. He lived a perfect life, was crucified to take the punishment for our sins, and conquered death by rising from the grave in newness of life. God the Father orchestrated all of this so that we—his beloved creation—could be reunited with him. No longer do our sins hold us back from relating with God but, as ***Hebrews 10:19-21 (MSG)*** declares, ***"we can now—without hesitation—walk right up to God, into 'the Holy Place.' Jesus has cleared the way by the blood of his sacrifice, acting as our priest before God. The 'curtain' into God's presence is his body."***

The *Holy Place* and *curtain* are references to the then temple of God: the place where God dwelt among his people under the Old Covenant. Only the high priest from the tribe of Levi, who had been ritually cleansed, could enter through a curtain into God's presence in the Holy Place. But now, through Jesus, we can have a freedom and a confidence to approach God at any time.

However, despite knowing this, Christians aren't immune to living a 'religious' Christian life. Just like all the other religions that don't claim man can be in union with God, we can so easily take our relationship with Jesus out of the equation. Instead of relying on the finished works of Christ to justify our relationship with God, we can go back to relying on our own works—a bit like collecting spiritual Brownie points.

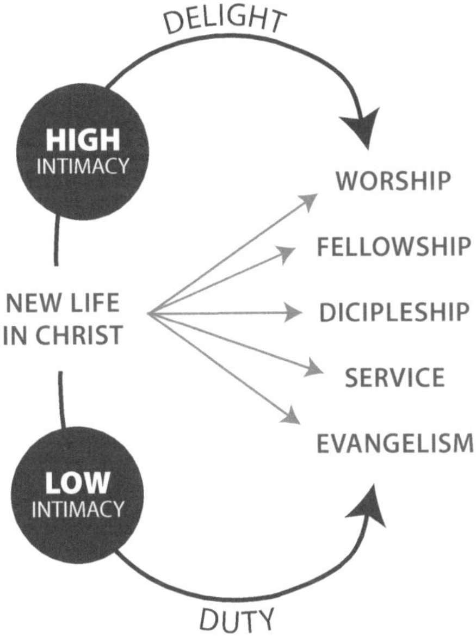

We can so easily end up forsaking, ignoring or forgetting the importance of our personal relationship with God. Instead of always being conscious of *being* a Christian, we focus on *doing* the things expected of Christians, such as attending church, reading our Bibles, serving others, going to prayer meetings and even sharing the gospel. But when that happens *we* become the focus, not *him*. We end up feeling guilty when we don't attend church; we take it personally when we don't serve well; we get disappointed when we miss a day reading our Bible; we feel ashamed when we don't share the gospel.

Whilst these are all commendable *good works*, when they are done out of duty rather than delight they don't exhibit holiness. Yes, if you're in Christ you're saved. Period. But if you don't keep your relationship with God as your prime focus then you can end up looking and acting like any follower of any other religion.

Remember, all other religions have to do good works to *reach God*, but we do good works because *God reached* us. Nothing is required of us to be saved, only faith in Christ. No small print. No clauses. It's all made possible through God's grace.

Although there's no list of rules and regulations that need to be kept to earn salvation, there are boundaries and expectations that will help us live a full life within our relationship with God.

When we are born again, it's not just a case of adding God into our life; we get added to his. He takes centre stage and we move out of the limelight. We don't boast that we're saved, but we boast that he is our Saviour. As ***1 Corinthians 1:31b*** (NLT) states, ***"If you want to boast, boast only about the Lord."***

The relationship we have with God is not like other religions that rely on relics or statues to remind them of their deities. In Christianity the Spirit of Christ enters our spirit with the prospect of consuming every part of our being. ***Acts 17:28 (AMP***) says, ***"For in Him we live and move and exist [that is, in Him we actually have our being], as even some of your own poets have said, 'For we also are His children.'"***

It's the 'in him' where we exist as Christians. Our born-again experience should be full of love for God, full of joy (that can be found even in times of sadness) and full of peace that surpasses all understanding.

QUESTIONS TO PONDER

- **Would your friends and family be surprised if you told them you had a personal relationship with God?**
- **If Jesus was living under your roof for a week in physical form, how would you relate to him differently to the way you do now?**
- **What Christian practices do you do more out of duty than delight? Why is that?**
- **If God wants you to approach him with confidence, what's stopping you? How can you eliminate that?**

YESTERDAY'S SUMMARY: Christianity stands out from all other religions because we have a personal relationship with a living God.

DAY 11

MILK & MEAT

IN SEVERAL PLACES, the Bible describes our relationship with God like a marriage. We (the Church) are the bride, and he is the groom. It also gives us another analogy of our relationship. Well, actually it's not just an analogy but also a reality: we are his children, he is our Father.

When we see this in the scriptures we can unpack so much from it; but one thing is clear. Just like a natural child has to mature, so do we grow spiritually. ***Luke 2:52 (NIVUK)*** tells us that even ***"Jesus grew in wisdom and stature, and in favour with God and man."***

At conversion we were literally 'born again'. We were spiritual babies. God fed us milk. ***1 Peter 2:2-3 (NIVUK)*** states, ***"Like newborn babies, crave pure spiritual milk, so that by it you may grow up in your salvation, now that you have tasted that the Lord is good."*** We get that wonderful taste of heaven that leads us to salvation and we desire more of the initial information that we were told in the gospel. So we grow as 'children' by learning and obeying the basics of Christianity.

In the natural there's a time when a boy becomes a man and a girl becomes a woman. Legally, it's normally around age 18 in the western world. In the east it can be lower; for instance, a Jewish child (like Jesus was) spiritually speaking becomes an adult at the age of 13. So it can depend on the place you live and the customs you hold to.

Biologically, the adolescent phase of a person as stated by the World Health Organization lasts between the ages of 10 and 19. During this period a child passes through puberty into a place where they can behave naturally as an adult. As in the natural, so in the spiritual. Now I'm not suggesting that every Christian has a nine-year period where they change from a spiritual child to an adult, but I *am* suggesting that there is a direct correlation.

There's a time in God when, after learning the basics as a child, we cross from childhood to adulthood. God may have a day in mind; it may be a time phase determined by our responses to those elementary truths—I don't know. But what I do know is that God treats us differently as spiritual adults than he does as spiritual children. And it's during this spiritual adolescent stage that many of us get stuck, because we assume God isn't going to say anything different to us than he has since we first knew him.

For example, your experience as a spiritual child is that God's divine providence has protected you from evil, but when God sees you're ready to act in the way of a spiritual adult he might say, 'Pick up the sword of the Spirit and fight for yourself in my name'. In the first instance he did it for us by his strength; in the second instance he asks us to do it in his strength. God's not lazy—he just doesn't want *us* to be. Nor is he double-minded; he just wants us to be sound-minded.

God doesn't want to push us around in a pram for the rest of our lives. He provides all the grace we need as a baby Christian, but when

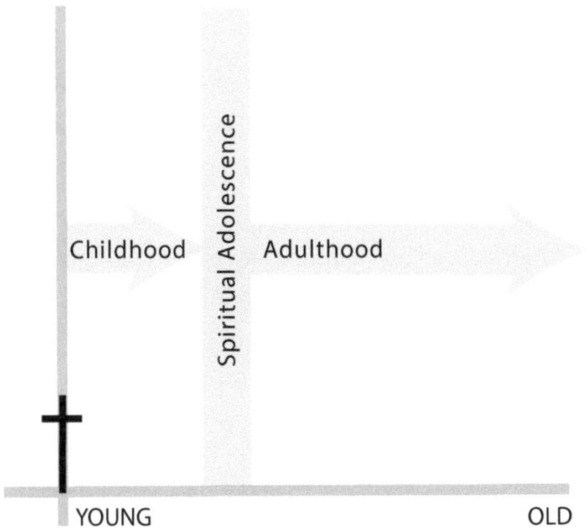

he knows that we're ready to stand on our own two feet he'll start by asking us to be obedient to his instructions. If you hardly ever read the Bible then you'll almost certainly still be drinking God's baby milk. You'll need lots of grace because you're not obeying his commands.

In ***Hebrews 5:11-12 (NLT),*** the struggling Christians are given some home truths: ***"you are spiritually dull and don't seem to listen. You have been believers so long now that you ought to be teaching others. Instead, you need someone to teach you again the basic things about God's word. You are like babies who need milk and cannot eat solid food."*** Again, the analogy of baby milk being like the basic teachings of Christ is used, but this time 'solid food' is introduced as a contrast.

The picture being painted is of adults walking around the church in nappies, sucking on dummies. They'd simply not grown as Christians because they didn't seem to listen. They didn't want to have a quiet time with God; they didn't want to go to the prayer meeting; they didn't pay attention to the sermon; they harboured unforgiveness and they didn't exercise faith. They were saved, but they didn't have Jesus as Lord.

We see a similar situation in ***1 Corinthians 3:1-3 (NIVUK)*** where the Apostle Paul address the church, ***"Brothers and sisters, I could not address you as people who live by the Spirit but as people who are still worldly – mere infants in Christ. I gave you milk, not solid food, for you were not yet ready for it. Indeed, you are still not ready. You are still***

worldly. For since there is jealousy and quarrelling among you, are you not worldly? Are you not acting like mere humans?" The believers were acting according to their old carnal nature instead of their new Spirit-inspired nature. God wasn't dishing out the meaty main course of the miraculous because they were struggling to manage the soup starter of simple instructions (my paraphrase!).

Conversely, there are times in our life when God tells us to do something we've never done before: forgive an enemy; increase our giving; share our faith with a particular person; read a certain book; take that job; leave that relationship—it could be a whole host of *next steps* in your journey into maturity. If you're not obedient, then you won't be able to grow in a particular area.

And sometimes these next steps not only turn a page of our life's story, but that page also concludes one chapter and starts a new one.

QUESTIONS TO PONDER

- **How well do you understand the doctrines of Christ such as repentance, faith, baptisms, laying on of hands, resurrection of the dead and eternal judgment?**
- **Where would you put yourself on the path of spiritual maturity that starts in childhood, goes through adolescence and continues through into adulthood?**
- **What was the last thing God told you to do? Have you done it? If not, why not, and when will you do it?**

YESTERDAY'S SUMMARY: God wants us to fully grasp the basic teachings of Christ, then move on to greater understanding so we can be used by him in greater ways.

DAY 12

THE CALL TO HOLINESS

1 PETER 1:13-16 (NLT) says, ***"So prepare your minds for action and exercise self-control. Put all your hope in the gracious salvation that will come to you when Jesus Christ is revealed to the world."*** Let's just pause there for a second to remind ourselves that Peter is talking here about the salvation *to come*. He then links it to us *being saved now*… ***"So you must live as God's obedient children. Don't slip back into your old ways of living to satisfy your own desires. You didn't know any better then. But now you must be holy in everything you do, just as God who chose you is holy. For the Scriptures say, 'You must be holy because I am holy'."*** There's one major thing we can get from these verses: Holiness is a commandment, not an option!

Holiness may feel like a lofty standard that's out of our reach, but God wouldn't tell us to pursue something that we couldn't attain.

So what is holiness? In the broader sense it means to *come apart*; to be *separate*. In the practical sense it means to be morally pure, free of sin. We have already been made holy because of the righteousness of Christ living inside our spirits, but we still need to walk in that holiness and manifest it in our lives.

Hebrews 10:14 (NIVUK), talking of Jesus, says that ***"by one sacrifice he has made perfect for ever those who are being made holy."*** Here we see the two views of holiness in one verse. We've *been* made perfect (positionally: in right-standing with God through Christ's perfect life having been sacrificed for us); we're *being* made perfect (relationally: morally pure through trusting and obeying God).

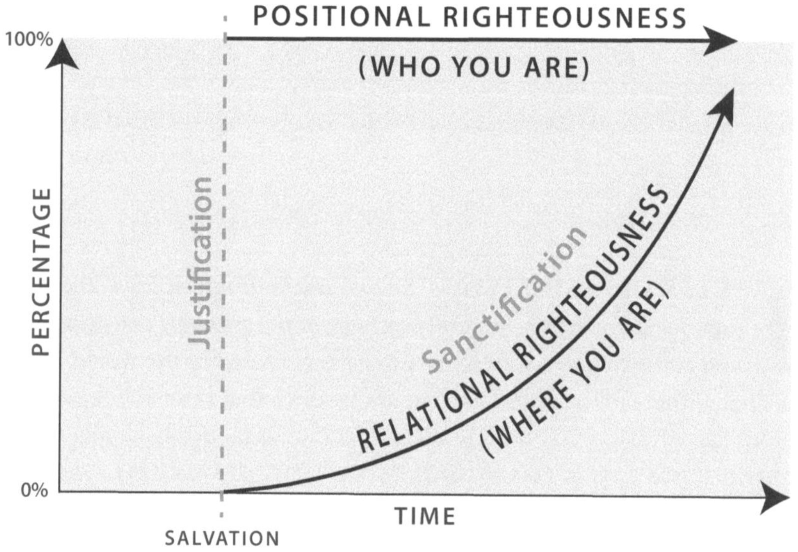

To help us wrap our head around this, let's look at the illustration above that shows two types of righteousness. There is positional righteousness based on *who we are* (as Christ is in us, we take on his righteousness). Then there is relational righteousness based on *where we are living* (either in the new Spirit nature or the old carnal nature).

Whilst living in this sin-trodden world with our carnal natures still lurking inside us, no one can be perfect in relational righteousness, although it should be our aim. This is where we are being perfected, and transformed through an intimate relationship with the perfecter of our faith (***Hebrews 12:2***). This is the lost art of being saved. There will always be things to work on in the future, but as long as we're being obedient to what God asks of us and are confessing our sins as they arise, then we'll get in on this amazing opportunity found in ***2 Timothy 2:21 (NLT),*** where Paul tells us, ***"If you keep yourself pure, you will be a special utensil for honourable use. Your life will be clean, and you will be ready for the Master to use you for every good work."*** God wants you to live in a continual state of purity where he can use you at any given time, for any good work!

Here is relational righteousness in action: Paul says in ***Philippians 3:12 (AMP), "Not that I have already obtained it [this goal of being Christlike] or have already been made perfect, but I actively press on so that I may take hold of that [perfection] for which Christ Jesus took hold of me and made me His own."***

The *process* of becoming holy is called sanctification. The *position* of having the righteousness of Christ is called justification.

Justified means 'just-as-if-I'd-never-sinned'. When God, the judge of heaven, looks at a born-again person he sees no consequence of sin in them because Christ has paid their penalty (that deserves a 'hallelujah' right there!) But *sanctification* is the process of becoming like the one who has named us. We are adopted by God into his royal family. All we need to do is embrace that by faith and walk appropriately in it.

Justification is about us *having been* saved, but holiness is about us *being* saved and will not be fully attained until Christ comes back again and we are *finally* saved.

The driver for *being* holy is the relationship that we have in Christ. ***2 Corinthians 7:1 (NLT)*** says, ***"Because we have these promises, dear friends, let us cleanse ourselves from everything that can defile our body or spirit. And let us work toward complete holiness because we fear God."***

We become holy by immersing ourselves in the holy scriptures, as we can see in ***Ephesians 5:25-26 (NLT): "Christ loved the church. He gave up his life for her to make her holy and clean, washed by the cleansing of God's word."***

If we're not becoming holy we're hindering ourselves from intimacy with God. We can't expect to have close fellowship with the Father when we're in disobedience. If we're walking in the Spirit, then we are being holy. However, if we're walking in the flesh, we're sinning. There's no third option.

The good news is that you don't *have* to sin! But when you do, you can confess it and repent of it. It's a lie to think that it's impossible to be holy.

Although there are no fast tracks in God, you can actually grow at a reasonable pace if you pursue holiness by following the Spirit's leading. You don't have to be a church minister or a theologian to be holy; you don't have to have been a Christian for decades for God to use you in a mighty way. You just need to walk in the Spirit, rather than the flesh. It might not always be easy, but it really is that simple.

QUESTIONS TO PONDER

- **How can knowing that you're fully righteous before God because of Jesus help you to become more righteous in your walk with him?**
- **What extra works do you think God might entrust you with if you were more 'set apart' for holiness than you are? And how can you improve in order to find out?**
- **In what way do you think that fearing God can help you to become more holy?**

YESTERDAY'S SUMMARY: You've been made perfect because of your position in Christ, but you are to be perfected in your performance.

DAY 13

CONSTANT PRESENCE

SOME PEOPLE HAVE never got to fully know their natural father growing up because he didn't stick around in their life. Others had only a limited time with them due to an early death. Still others don't even know who their fathers are because their mother's pregnancy was a result of casual sex, maybe even rape. Life is not fair sometimes and can be devastating for people who have no control over such circumstances.

The good news, however, is that we have a perfect *heavenly* Father who is always with us. He will never leave us or forsake us; he longs to be ever present in our lives. But herein lies probably the biggest deficit that a Christian can experience whilst being saved: the lack of God's presence.

When it comes to sensing God, the strategic thinking of many Christians is to get a spiritual fix during a Sunday service, maybe also in a midweek small group, and a morning devotion wherever they can.

After this they switch themselves into *natural* mode, not expecting much more outside those times. Yet life in God is not meant to be experienced through irregular events, but rather through a continual process.

If I only ever spoke to Kate between the hours of 6 and 7am, or only on Sunday mornings, not only would that be weird but it would also put a strain on our marriage. We shouldn't think it's any different with God. Relationships are built on communication. Even when we can't speak to a loved one in person, we'll at least try phoning or texting—we'll do whatever it takes. We should pursue God with the same resolve.

Below is my best attempt at illustrating how a Christian might spend their time in the presence of God during a typical week (shown by the dark grey areas). There may actually be some random thoughts and prayers scattered throughout any given day, but let's use this simplified diagram to at least make a point.

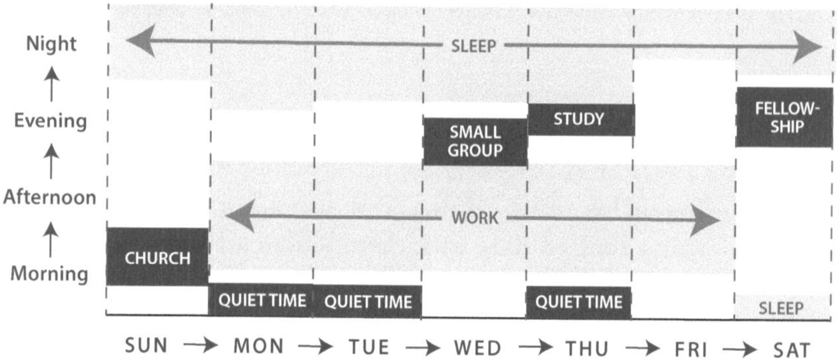

In this scenario, we only see around 12 hours of our 168-hour week with any real intent towards being in the presence of God. This represents only seven per cent of the time we give to him, when he has made himself available to us 100 per cent of the time.

I'm guessing there's a fair chance right now that you may want to draw my attention to the big time-filling light grey blocks of work and sleep that you can't do much about. Together they equate to a whopping 60 per cent of your week. Let me make a couple of quick points regarding these.

Firstly, sleep. Your mind is still active when you're out with the fairies; you're just not conscious (hence the ability to dream). And because God never sleeps nor slumbers, this is potentially a lost opportunity for him to speak to you through dreams if you don't prepare yourself for this. Even a short prayer every night that invites God to protect your mind from evil thoughts and speak to you during the watches of the night can pay huge dividends. There are also great apps out there to guide you in settling your soul and consciously engaging your spirit with God during your last moments awake. If we know the benefit of starting our day with intentional quiet times, why wouldn't we start six, seven or eight hours of sleep with the same intent?

Secondly, work. Obviously we can't be using work time for our personal godly pursuits, but we're told in scripture to serve our employers as if we were serving the Lord (***Ephesians 6:5***), so we should have a level of Christ-consciousness as we work each day. And the fact is, the Holy Spirit is inside us so we take him to work anyway. We just need to be mindful of this as we go about our days.

Then there are the white areas on the diagram that are uncategorised. These represent a significant 33 per cent of our time that is taken up by the mundane, everyday tasks of life. We all have to wash (ourselves, our clothes and the dishes!), we have houses to upkeep, families to attend to, finances to organise—the list could go on. But the same question arises: how can we habitually include God in these situations?

I probably spend around one hour a day walking to local meetings. Sometimes I utilise the time to catch up on texts and emails, but wherever I don't have to do that I try and use the time to speak in tongues or to pray. Whether you're walking, driving or on the bus, train or bike, this is a great opportunity to converse with your Creator.

If we're intentional and creative in our thinking, we can invite a lot more of God into our week than we think. You could binge read a book rather than a Netflix series. You could listen to worship music whilst doing the ironing. How about sending an encouraging text to someone rather than checking your social media notifications? And, without wanting to be crude, every time you sit on the loo you could spend that time in prayer. Sometimes in our frantically paced world of distractions, we need triggers to help us get back into a realm of God-consciousness.

But remember, we're not just trying to add *events*; we're trying to utilise opportunities to build up to a continual process where we're always in a position to hear God. Whilst Christ is in *us*, there is still a call of scripture for us to be in *him*. Without this, we end up going through the motions and not being fruitful or productive in our lives—as ***John 15:4 (NIVUK)*** says, ***"Remain in me, as I also remain in you. No branch can bear fruit by itself; it must remain in the vine. Neither can you bear fruit unless you remain in me."***

All of this won't happen by accident. It takes intent; it takes routine; it takes persistence. There will always be distractions or seemingly better offers for your time. Be easy on yourself. Don't let condemnation sneak in. Start small. God sees your heart, he understands your situation and he'll help you to increase his presence in your life.

QUESTIONS TO PONDER

- **Based on the illustration given, if you had to guess roughly how many hours you intentionally spend with God each week what would that be?**
- **What could you do to bring more of God into your time at work and your time asleep?**
- **What one routine of life could you plan to involve God in during the next seven days?**
- **How do you feel about the fact that God longs to spend time with you, occupying your whole mind and life?**

◀◀ **YESTERDAY'S SUMMARY:** God doesn't want to just spend small amounts of quality time with you; he wants to be an ever-present reality.

DAY 14

EXERCISE FAITH

WITHOUT FAITH, IT'S not *difficult* to please God; it's *impossible*! Everything we do needs to be infused with faith, believing for God to come through on each and every promise he makes.

If we're living the full life marked out for us in Christ, then we need to be walking constantly by faith in the spiritual realm rather than by sight in the natural realm. ***2 Corinthians 5:7 (NLT)*** echoes this sentiment: ***"we live by faith, not by sight."*** And ***Romans 10:17 (NLT)*** tells us that faith comes from the Word of God. ***"So faith comes from hearing, that is, hearing the Good News about Christ".*** So intimacy requires a regular engagement with Jesus revealed through the holy scriptures.

It still astounds me that Christians are so deceived into thinking that their lack of intimacy with the scriptures is not directly linked to their lack of intimacy with God. Jesus himself *is* the Word. ***John 1:14 (AMP)*** tells us that, ***"the Word (Christ) became flesh, and lived among us."***

God wants you to have faith in him, to trust him to direct your every step, every day of your life. ***Hebrews 11:1 (NLT)*** declares, ***"Faith shows the reality of what we hope for; it is the evidence of things we cannot see."*** Faith is simply trusting God to do what he said he would do.

You can't get intimate with God without believing that God wants intimacy with you, and that you have full access to him through the finished work of Christ.

An end goal of this six-week journey is to get you to a place where you start relying on God's voice for every decision you need to make—whether it's something major like a house move, new job or potential marriage, or something more mundane, like what to eat and maybe even what to wear.

This isn't all going to happen imminently; it takes a lifelong quest of God and he reveals more and more to us as our trust in him increases. But we *can* make significant strides by the end of the time we have together.

Like in the diagram below, your life has probably seen various ups and downs as you've worked out how to *be* saved. There might have

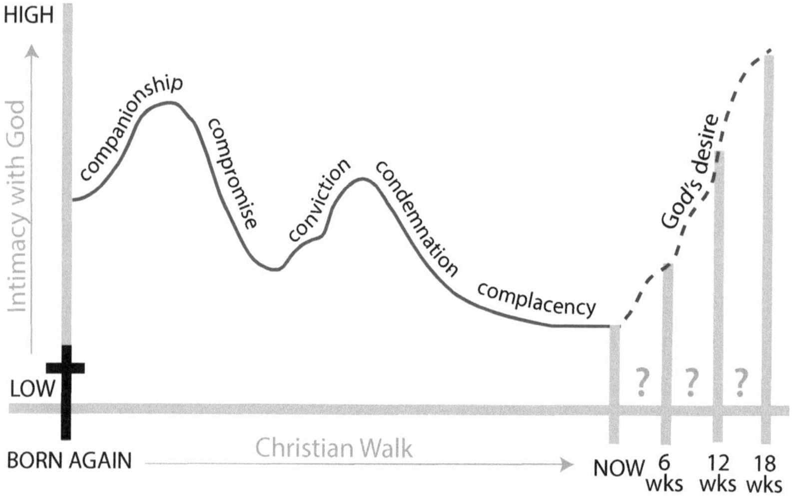

been bumps in the road that have caused you to stumble. It may have all started well in the beginning when everything was new and your relationship with God became increasingly real. Maybe after a while the devil tempted you to go back to some of your old worldly ways and you ended up making compromises that you didn't want to make. But at some stage the convicting work of the Holy Spirit came to your aid and pulled you back on track.

Then, inevitably, you slipped back again, with condemnation having free rein in your mind to act as some kind of self-appointed punishment. And perhaps you learned to live with it and settled for a life of complacency that you're living now—knowing you're saved but content with a limited level of intimacy with God.

If that even vaguely represents your life in Christ, then I've got two words from heaven for you: go again! God knew you'd fall back again at some point, but this time he wants you to trust him and get straight back up again. He wants your company. Not later today. Not tomorrow. Not next term or next year. But *now*.

Even within just a few weeks, you can reach new heights in God; you can break the back of this new life of intimacy, this art of being saved. You can start to hear God in ways you never thought possible; you can gain great momentum that can set you up for the rest of your life.

Don't let the devil say you're not good enough; don't let condemnation counter the desires of God. What decent father wouldn't want to see his children succeed and prosper in life? Just as God loved his Son Jesus, now he loves you, too.

You may have been a Christian for decades and feel like you've blown it with God. Rubbish! That's a lie from the pit of hell. You may not have grown as much as God wanted you to, but nothing is wasted in him. He can even use your past mistakes to help others in similar situations. In fact, in studying the themes I'm presenting, I've felt that I've wasted time myself, that I've not reached the potential God had for me within the time I've been given. But, in having that reality check, I can write this book to help prevent others from making the same mistakes, enabling them to have a better start in their journey with God.

A closer, more consistent relationship with God is the heartbeat of being saved. It seems out of reach in the natural mind, but it's fully possible.

James 4:7-8 (NLT) says, ***"humble yourselves before God. Resist the devil, and he will flee from you. Come close to God, and God will come close to you"*** (emphasis mine). This is such a powerful verse. By eliminating pride and saying *no* to what opposes God, you can actually move the Creator of the cosmos towards you! Just take a moment now and imagine God getting off his throne and walking in your direction. He's approaching with intent; he's closing in for fellowship; he's bringing with him love, acceptance and forgiveness.

James 2:26 (NLT) tells us, ***"Just as the body is dead without breath, so also faith is dead without good works."*** Faith demands an accompanying action. Why not take a moment and actively engage in an encounter with the living God?

QUESTIONS TO PONDER

- **In what practical ways could you demonstrate your belief that God wants to reveal more of his will and purpose for your life?**
- **Do you recognise a similar pattern in your life to the one on today's diagram? If so, what part in particular?**
- **Can you believe for your relationship with God to be far more intimate by the end of this book than it is now? What might try and get in the way of that? And how can you stop it?**

WEEK 2 SUMMARY

Day 8: Thriving or Surviving? – Egypt was a land of 'not enough', the wilderness was a land of 'just enough', but the Promised Land was a land of 'more than enough'. Jesus died so you could live in the Promised Land.

Day 9: Born on Purpose – We were saved by God's good works in order to do good works for him, which he prepared for us long ago.

Day 10: Religion vs Relationship – Christianity stands out from all other religions because we have a personal relationship with the living God.

Day 11: Milk & Meat – God wants us to fully grasp the basic teachings of Christ, but move on to deeper understanding so we can be used by him in greater ways.

Day 12: The Call to Holiness – You've been made perfect because of your position in Christ, but you are to be perfected in your performance.

Day 13: Constant Presence – God doesn't want to just spend small amounts of quality time with you; he wants to be an ever-present reality.

Day 14: Exercise Faith – You can reach new heights in God if you believe that's what he desires for you.

Your flesh can't
be cleansed; it must
be crucified.

WEEK
3

Our opposition to intimacy:
SELF

HEART ISSUES

The human heart pumps blood round our body, keeping us alive. So too the blood of Jesus has made us alive spiritually. But just as our natural hearts can experience complications, our spiritual hearts can also.

As I've already mentioned, I began writing this book as part of a three-month sabbatical—one where I unfortunately was twice blue-lighted into hospital with a racing heartbeat, which was diagnosed as atrial fibrillation (AF).

We're going to look into the basic function of this vital organ a little more in a later chapter, so we can see how the heart keeps a regular rhythm and how it's crucial that we do the same spiritually.

But as I experienced—as we all do to some degree, whether knowingly or unknowingly—there are various factors that can contribute to dicky hearts. In my case, it was malfunctioning cells sending rogue electrical signals that they weren't designed to do.

A NEW HEART

Now when the Bible talks about the heart it rarely refers to our physical blood pump; it normally means the immaterial heart of a person—their soul, the centre of their being; the place where emotions, intellect and desires are conceived. For instance, ***1 Corinthians 4:5 (NIVUK)*** says that ***"the Lord will bring to light what is hidden in darkness and will expose the motives of the heart." Proverbs 16:23 (NIVUK)*** tells us, ***"The hearts of the wise make their mouths prudent, and their lips promote instruction."*** And ***Romans 10:9 (NIVUK)*** says that we ***"believe in our hearts"***. So we can see that the 'heart' has motives, as well as producing wisdom and belief.

As prophesied in the Old Testament and fulfilled in the New Testament, when anyone believes in him God allows their heart to become new. No longer must we have hard, sin-focused hearts that were created by our own selfish desires, but we can now experience soft, pliable hearts that can be moulded and shaped by the Spirit and the ways of God.

A SICK HEART

But just like my human heart was sick, so too our spiritual hearts can be. ***Jeremiah 17:9 (AMP)*** states, ***"The heart is deceitful above all things. And it is extremely sick; Who can understand it fully and know its secret motives?"*** Jesus himself echoed this sentiment in ***Mark 7:21 (NLT)*** when he said, ***"For from within, out of a person's heart, come evil thoughts, sexual immorality, theft, murder, adultery, greed, wickedness, deceit, lustful desires, envy, slander, pride, and foolishness."***

Although we have the new life of God in our spirits that totally transforms us, we can still wilfully disconnect it and reconnect to our old, fleshly nature. (If this concept is still new to you, it might be worth reviewing the teaching in Day 3, or at least the diagram.)

Just like the rogue heart tissue was causing chaos with my heart rhythms—which in turn caused difficulty in my breathing—our old nature can interfere with our new life in God if we go back to it in any way, shape or form. Although this is abnormal behaviour for a Christian, it's easily done. The old nature opposes itself against every way of the Spirit. ***Galatians 5:25 (NIVUK)*** says, ***"Since we live by the Spirit, let us keep in step with the Spirit."***

HEART TREATMENT

Going back to the physical condition, the answer for many with AF is to have minor, non-invasive surgery called an *ablation*. A catheter is inserted into a major artery—normally through the groin area up into the heart. There it maps out the problem areas of the heart before burning small areas that stop the electrical signals interfering. We too have to take fairly drastic action with our fleshly desires and actions if we want to breathe properly spiritually. ***Colossians 3:5 (NIVUK)*** says it like this: ***"Put to death, therefore, whatever belongs to your earthly nature."*** Strong but necessary language if we're going to *be* saved as God designed us to.

But how do you kill something spiritually? Well, we can start to get an answer from ***Philippians 2:1-8 (MSG)***; it begins by presenting the following scenario, which every believer falls into in some way: ***"If you've gotten anything at all out of following Christ, if his love has made any difference in your life, if being in a community of the Spirit means anything to you, if you have a heart, if you care—then do me a favor:"***

The next few verses give us a list of treatments that we can take to heal a sick spiritual heart. Here they are: ***"Agree with each other, love each other, be deep-spirited friends. Don't push your way to the front; don't sweet-talk your way to the top. Put yourself aside, and help others get ahead. Don't be obsessed with getting your own advantage. Forget yourselves long enough to lend a helping hand."*** In short: don't be led by yourself, be led by the Spirit.

The instructions conclude with an encouragement to jump into the mind of Christ and get a perspective from there. ***"Think of yourselves the way Christ Jesus thought of himself. He had equal status with God but didn't think so much of himself that he had to cling to the advantages of that status no matter what. Not at all. When the time came, he set aside the privileges of deity and took on the status of a slave, became human! Having become human, he stayed human. It was an incredibly humbling process. He didn't claim special privileges. Instead, he lived a selfless, obedient life and then died a selfless, obedient death—and the worst kind of death at that—a crucifixion."***

So we should live with less of self and more of God. Sounds right, but many struggle to achieve this for various reasons—deception, I believe, being the major one.

UNDIAGNOSED ISSUES

The National Library of Medicine has estimated that up to 40 per cent of people with AF don't realise they have it. It's normally picked up whilst treating other conditions. How similar this is to the Church today. Many new creations in Christ are walking around with fleshly lifestyles—and a significant amount of them don't even know it!

So this coming week we're going to look into how the devil deceives us in this way. We'll also look into how pride causes all kinds of problems in our hearts, as well as how we can get back in step with the Holy Spirit through the convictions he brings and the empowerment he gives us to overcome.

All that and more to come, so let's get started…

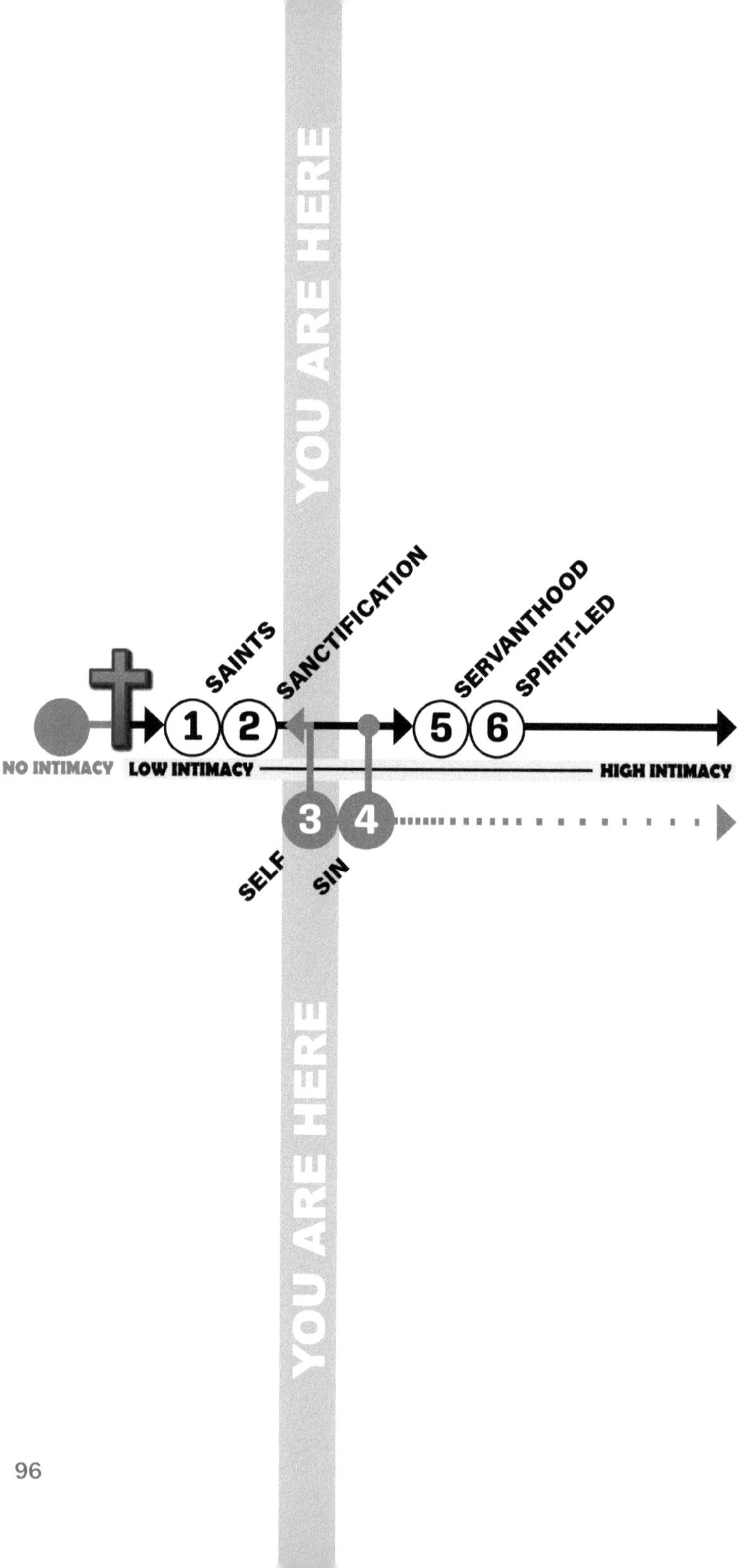
YOU ARE HERE
SAINTS
SANCTIFICATION
SERVANTHOOD
SPIRIT-LED
1
2
5
6
NO INTIMACY
LOW INTIMACY
HIGH INTIMACY
3
4
SELF
SIN
YOU ARE HERE

DAY 15

CARNAL LIVING

THE CHURCH AT Corinth had a number of problems in its formative years. The Apostle Paul planted this church on his first missionary journey. He lived with them for around a year and a half, before moving on to establish further churches. Unfortunately, it didn't take long for these new believers to conform again to the patterns of the world around them.

Quite a lot was kicking off: favouritism, sleeping around, racial issues, disruptions in church services, and important differences on 'end-time' teachings. Paul got wind of this and wrote them a letter to bring some order and clarity. In it he calls out their immaturity, their worldliness and their carnality: ***1 Corinthians 3:3 (AMP)*** says, ***"You are still worldly [controlled by ordinary impulses, the sinful capacity]. For as long as there is jealousy and strife and discord among you, are you not unspiritual, and are you not walking like ordinary men [unchanged by faith]?"***

As we discovered last week, God's desire is for us to be sanctified; we achieve this through obedience to the Spirit. When we accept Christ, the power of the flesh is cut off and we no longer have to draw from that nature. Because we're still human and many worldly behaviours are habitual, it can take time to bring them all under control. But the idea is that when we become born again we immediately start drawing from the Spirit, resulting in the times we act in the flesh becoming fewer and fewer.

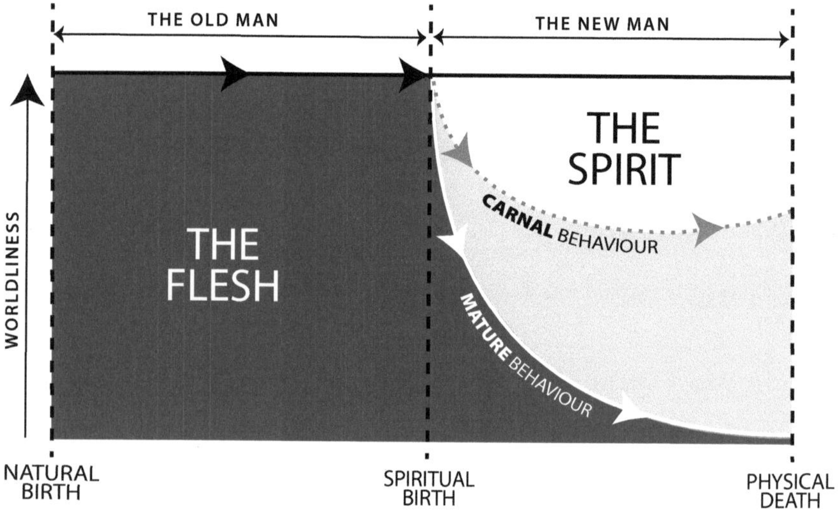

This wasn't the case with the Corinthian church. And, sad to say, it's not always the case in your church or mine.

As Christians we should stand out from people of the world. We saw last week that we are called to be holy. 'Holy' means to be *set apart*. It also means to be *different*. When visitors walk into a church building they should see something totally different, something counter-cultural. I'm glad to say that this was my experience some 30 years ago when I got involved in church life. It was actually the catalyst for me seeking God further and, soon after, being saved.

And I'm glad to say that, even today, different churches that I'm connected to or am aware of, by and large, are good adverts for the Kingdom of God. Of course no one belongs to a perfect church (if you do, you need to leave because you're making it imperfect!), but when something of the authentic, loving nature of Jesus is manifested within a group of wildly diverse people, all finding common ground in Christ, it's a powerful and wonderfully effective way of drawing others to the Kingdom. It's the answer to part of Jesus' priestly prayer in ***John 17:20-21 (NIVUK), "I pray also for those who will believe in me through their message, that all of them may be one, Father, just as you are in me and I am in you. May they also be in us so that the world may believe that you have sent me."***

God's idea of the Church is the most beautiful idea when you see it working as intended. Conversely, when it's not it can be a bad advert for Christianity. ***Galatians 5:9 (NIVUK)*** says that ***"A little yeast works through the whole batch of dough."*** Quarrels in the corridors, unspoken unforgiveness and bad attitudes are just some of the bits of 'yeast' that can, if not challenged and repented of, work their way through the whole batch of dough (meaning 'body of believers'), bringing divisions that can even lead to the heartrending reality of church splits.

What preventative measure can we take to minimise any such eventuality? Deny yourself, think of others before yourself, confess your sins and change your ways, love your neighbour—there's a few for starters. But here's the solution in a nutshell: follow the Spirit of God, not your carnal desires. In ***Luke 9:23 (NLT)*** Jesus says, ***"If any of you wants to be my follower, you must give up your own way, take up your cross daily, and follow me".***

It seems to me that, in this day and age, far too many people attending our churches could be labelled 'carnal Christians' judging by their lifestyles. Are they in fact born again at all? I don't know. It's not for me to judge. But some appear to treat church like a social club. Some check in every now and again on a Sunday to keep their membership alive. Others speak negatively about the worship as if the songs were for their personal enjoyment. Outside the four walls of the church building, some are seen at parties having drunk too much. Some have been living in unforgiveness for decades. And others are living with unmarried partners because 'that's what people do these days'.

This all grieves God deeply and is proof that, although local churches should aspire to be beacons of light in a carnal world, they still have the capacity to display worldliness. ***Romans 12:2 (NIVUK)*** instructs us, ***"Do not conform to the pattern of this world".***

I'll leave you today with these sobering words of Jesus in ***Matthew 7:21-23 (NLT)*** as he talks about false prophets and so-called Christians. Just as you can identify a tree by its fruit, so you can identify people by their actions. ***"Not everyone who calls out to me, 'Lord! Lord!' will enter the Kingdom of Heaven. Only those who actually do the will of my Father in heaven will enter. On judgement day many will say to me, 'Lord! Lord! We prophesied in your name and cast out demons in your name and performed many miracles in your name.' But I will reply, 'I never knew you. Get away from me, you who break God's laws.'"***

This is certainly not the book to have a 'once saved, always saved' debate, but my current belief is that those Jesus is referring to are not people who are actually saved, but people who believe they are saved based on *the company they kept* rather than *their faith in Christ.*

QUESTIONS TO PONDER

- In what ways do you think your unsaved family, friends and colleagues see that you're different?
- Do you blend into a non-Christian crowd, or do you stand out? In what ways?
- What publicly known sin have you experienced in your local church or have you seen reported in another church in the news? What effect did it have?
- In what ways do you see carnality/worldliness creeping into the Church today?

YESTERDAY'S SUMMARY: Certain lifestyles within the Church are a bad advert for God. Christians need to understand they're living according to their old nature, and make a change.

DAY 16

CHOICES, CHOICES

LIFE IS INCREASINGLY becoming crammed with choices for us to make. There's so much to decide on: what we're going to think, wear, eat, watch, avoid, read, select, pay, say, hear, check… (and all the multiple variations within each activity).

A Psychology Today blog suggested that we actually make an eye-popping 35,000 choices a day. That equates to around 2,000 per waking hour! Now you may be screwing your face up at this, sarcastically saying 'yeah, right', but when you think that the majority of decisions made are subconscious then it might not actually be that far out.

When we were born again we didn't get transported out of this world. We still have to navigate it, along with all the decisions it presents to us. But as Christians we should now be charting our course in a totally different direction. The choices we now make should be based on a Kingdom perspective, not the old worldly perspective we were used to. For instance, we now choose truth over lies, good over evil, love over hate, diligence over laziness and humility over pride. In reality, when you boil it all down, we're left with just two categories of choice: decisions based on the Spirit and decisions based on the flesh. One is obedience and one is disobedience. There's no middle ground.

The mind that is presented with all our choices can be illustrated somewhat by looking at how we use a computer. Let's break it down...

THE COMPUTER contains both the hardware (e.g. the processor) and the software (e.g. the programs) to run everything. It's all working away in the background without us even realising it. This is like our subconscious mind. When you were saved, God installed a brand new operating system inside you. ***2 Corinthians 5:17 (NLT)*** says, ***"anyone who belongs to Christ has become a new person. The old life is gone; a new life has begun!"***

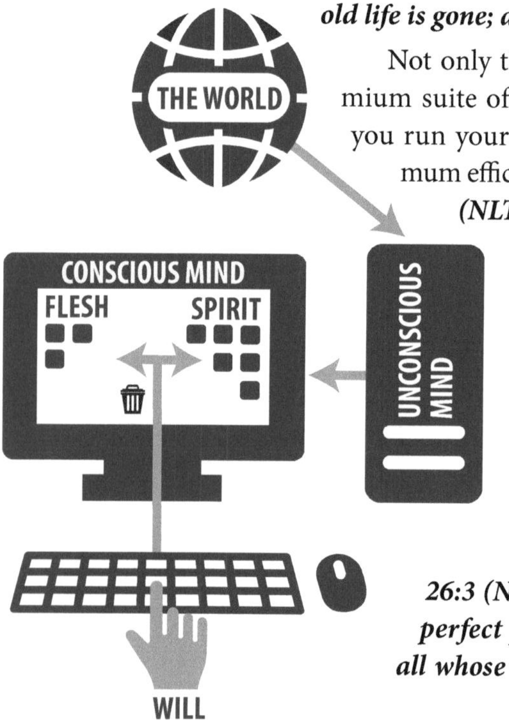

Not only that, but he loaded up a premium suite of heavenly programs to help you run your new life in Christ to maximum efficiency, as we see in ***2 Peter 1:3 (NLT): "By his divine power, God has given us everything we need for living a godly life."***

THE SCREEN shows you what you need to know about what's inside the computer so that you can use it how you want. It represents your conscious mind, what you're focusing on. ***Isaiah 26:3 (NLT)*** reads, ***"You will keep in perfect peace all who trust in you, all whose thoughts are fixed on you!"***

And ***Philippians 4:8 (NLT)*** says, ***"Fix your thoughts on what is true, and honorable, and right, and pure, and lovely, and admirable. Think about things that are excellent and worthy of praise."***

THE DESKTOP has shortcuts to our most used programs. They can be Spirit-based apps that help us, or flesh-based apps that hinder us. Within the former group are some of those new programs that God installed. The basic *starter* ones have been pre-installed ready for us. ***1 Corinthians 3:2 (NIVUK)*** says, ***"I gave you milk, not solid food, for you were not yet ready for it."***

As mentioned, a wealth of other programs are accessible in the computer. Unfortunately we just don't realise that through ignorance, or because we haven't yet mastered the basic programs. ***Hebrews 5:11-12 (MSG)*** speaks of such a scenario, ***"By this time you ought to be teachers yourselves, yet here I find you need someone to sit down with you and go over the basics on God again, starting from square one—baby's milk, when you should have been on solid food long ago!"***

THE TRASH/BIN folder is where you put unnecessary, unwanted and irrelevant files. You could say that this is where the record of our sins go when we've confessed them. God doesn't look at the trash/bin—***Hebrews 8:12 (NLT)*** tells us, ***"I will forgive their wickedness, and I will never again remember their sins."*** He doesn't need to access this folder because the consequences related to it were dealt with two millennia ago. ***1 Peter 2:24 (NLT)*** says, ***"He personally carried our sins in his body on the cross so that we can be dead to sin and live for what is right. By his wounds you are healed."***

THE WORLD we live in is here represented by 'internet access'. Even as new creations, we can still be influenced by the patterns of the world. ***Romans 12:2 (NIVUK)*** says, ***"Do not conform to the pattern of this world, but be transformed by the renewing of your mind. Then you will be able to test and approve what God's will is – his good, pleasing and perfect will."*** When we choose to go back and adopt old ways of living we can end up downloading old fleshly programs. These come with new shortcuts on our desktops and we start operating them like we used to do—often without realising it.

THE OPERATOR is you. You choose which keys to press and what part of the screen you click on. Those thousands of choices you make every day are all based on how you think.

Programs don't run by themselves; you choose to open them. To our detriment, we can choose to run the new, worldly programs—we can even go back and retrieve the old files and apps. The devil wants us to do that and remind us of our past; he wants us to be exposed to the virus of condemnation. That's why ***1 Peter 5:8 (NLT)*** warns us to "***Stay alert! Watch out for your great enemy, the devil. He prowls around like a roaring lion, looking for someone to devour.***"

The best thing we can do in that situation is put those files back where they belong and run our antivirus program that scans our heart and quarantines any fleshly files. Then we can hit the refresh button by applying ***James 4:7 (NIVUK),*** which instructs us, ***"Submit yourselves, then, to God. Resist the devil, and he will flee from you."***

QUESTIONS TO PONDER

- **When was the last time you consciously chose the Spirit over the flesh? What was it about and what happened as a result?**
- **How aware are you of the subconscious decisions you make?**
- **How easy is it for you to keep your mind fixed on Jesus? What one thing distracts you the most? How can you lessen this or eliminate it?**

YESTERDAY'S SUMMARY: How you think determines the choices you make. The choices you make determine the actions you take.

DAY 17

PERSONAL CONVICTIONS

WHILST ON OUR recent sabbatical Kate and I decided to watch a Netflix series. More than anything, the reason was to spend some time together.

We love a drama (theatrically speaking), so got through a few of those in the first few weeks. I love a true story as well. That drew me to the newly released *Dahmer*. Well, based on the first episode it was more akin to a horror than a drama. The series is about the story of serial killer and sex offender Jeffry Dahmer who, between 1978 and 1991, murdered and dismembered 17 men and boys. (Interestingly, Dahmer found Jesus in prison—that would make fascinating viewing if documented on screen.)

After that opening episode we both woke up in the middle of the night having bad dreams, and in the morning we both simultaneously knew that God didn't approve of us watching and didn't want us to continue with the series. ***2 Corinthians 6:14 (NIVUK)*** was a verse circulating in our spirits: "***what fellowship can light have with darkness?***" The rest of the episodes may have been much milder, they may have been less horrific—I don't know. But that didn't matter. What did matter was that we were sensitive to the Holy Spirit and obedient to his instruction. I'm not saying it's wrong to watch this series or anything else like it; what I'm saying is that you won't know what's right or wrong for you unless you're tuned into the frequency of the Holy Spirit.

As you mature in God, and as you spend more time in his presence, he will unsettle you where you need to be unsettled. The key then is to follow that through to obedience.

A few years ago we were at the local cinema. We love a trip there with the huge, wide screen, comfortably seated in the reclining black leather chairs with popcorn poised on our laps. But five minutes into this film and there was constant foul language and a graphic sex scene. I think we both knew at this point that we shouldn't be watching. Kate gave an initial suggestion that we should leave, but it took me another 15 minutes to reach her level of godliness, and turn to her with a gesture towards the exit. We walked out in front of everyone. Disobeying the Holy Spirit wasn't an option.

On another occasion I felt God tell me to stop listening to the radio in the car because it just wasn't edifying. Now I love my music as much as the next person, but I would have sinned if I had kept on listening—***James 4:17 (NIVUK)*** points out, ***"If anyone, then, knows the good they ought to do and doesn't do it, it is sin for them."*** Similarly, ***Romans 14:23 (NLT)*** in the context of the early Christians' dilemma about whether they should eat food that had been sacrificed to idols, says, ***"if you have doubts about whether or not you should eat something, you are sinning if you go ahead and do it. For you are not following your convictions. If you do anything you believe is not right, you are sinning."***

We could have carried on watching the Netflix series; after all, no one else would know. We could have justified staying in the cinema; after all, other people were there (and I bet some of them were Christians). I didn't have to turn the car radio off; after all, it wasn't affecting anyone else—and the tunes were quite catchy (well, some of them).

If you're walking in the Spirit, you'll get a check in your spirit when the Holy Spirit is convicting you. The peace of God will depart. You'll feel slightly uncomfortable at first, and if you don't block it out, it'll keep niggling away at you. Not only that, but God can confirm the situation through scripture for you, like he did with us over the Dahmer series.

The thing is, we can't be only partially obedient. You're either in the cinema still or you've left. And turning the radio volume down isn't obedience when the Holy Spirit says turn it off.

In ***Romans 7:18 (AMP)*** the great Apostle Paul illustrates the battle many of us have when we invite Jesus as Saviour, but don't choose him as Lord (Master). He says, ***"For I know that nothing good lives in me, that is, in my flesh [my human nature, my worldliness—my sinful capacity]. For the willingness [to do good] is present in me, but the doing of good is not."***

So you need to totally and utterly reject your old nature. Don't compromise! Don't enter into negotiations. Turn completely away from it. Kill it!! ***Colossians 3:5-10 (NLT)*** puts it like this: ***"So put to death the sinful, earthly things lurking within you. Have nothing to do with sexual immorality, impurity, lust, and evil desires. Don't be greedy, for a greedy person is an idolater, worshiping the things of this world. Because of these sins, the anger of God is coming. You used to do these things when your life was still part of this world. But now is the time to get rid of anger, rage, malicious behavior, slander, and dirty language. Don't lie to each other, for you have stripped off your old sinful nature and all its wicked deeds. Put on your new nature, and be renewed as you learn to know your Creator and become like him."***

It's a process. You're identified by the full righteousness of God in your innermost being; you're sealed by the Spirit; you're set apart for good works. But you have to hear the personal convictions in your spirit; you can only do this as you walk with the Holy Spirit.

We often assume something is right when God says it's wrong. Conversely, something can be okay when we think it's not. These kinds of things are always close to the Spirit/flesh divide, as illustrated below. In the ideal world we're living in all righteousness, but for the times that we cross over into the flesh we just need to be obedient.

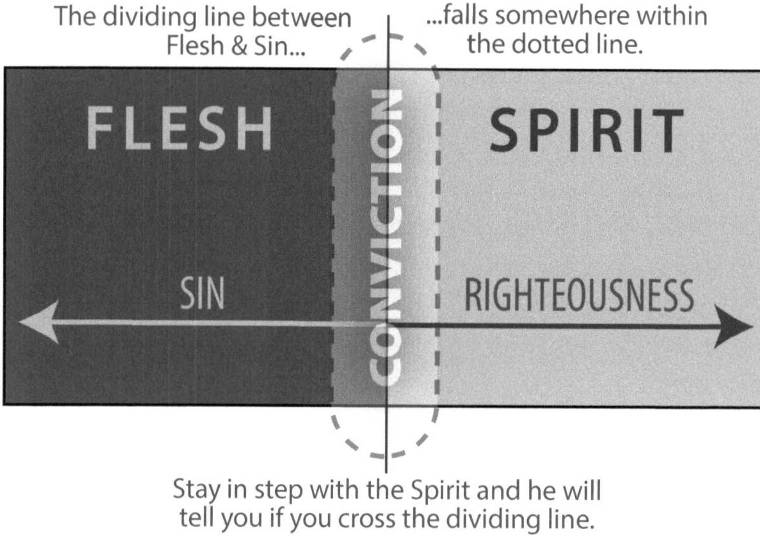

QUESTIONS TO PONDER

- **When did you last get convicted to do something, or not to do something? Did you follow through? If you did, how did it go? If you didn't, what stopped you?**
- **Would you sense the Holy Spirit convict you if he needed to? If not, why not?**
- **In what ways do you sense the conviction of the Holy Spirit? How can you tell that it's him?**

YESTERDAY'S SUMMARY: God convicts us of our sin when we first come to him. After that, he convicts us of what is right and wrong for us personally.

DAY 18

EXPOSING DECEPTION

AS WE CONTINUE to look at the two opposing natures vying for our attention, it's important to understand that there is no *middle ground* or *neutral area* between them.

One of the greatest deceptions of Satan is, 'You might not be doing anything good, but neither are you doing anything bad'. However, the truth of the matter is that you're always doing one or the other in God's eyes, because you can only act out of one nature or the other!

As Christians we're either walking in the ways of the *world* or the ways of the *Kingdom*. They are two totally different domains. Many Christians imagine that there is some kind of neutral zone that God is okay with. A place where they may not be evangelising to multitudes or raising the dead, but equally they're not doing anything seriously wrong.

This is a dangerous place to be as a Christian. Firstly, because it's a place of deceit, and secondly because it's a comfortable place to be, with no growth potential. It's also a place to tread carefully because this is where backsliding starts. You may not be hurting anyone, but you're incredibly vulnerable.

Your enemy the devil can't do anything about the work of salvation inside you, but he loves to get you in that place of deceit because it's there that you become complacent; it's there that discipline is slack. Suddenly it doesn't matter if you miss church or you don't read your Bible as much. After all, you're still a Christian and God loves you. That may be true, but God is not always happy and the Holy Spirit can be grieved!

Whereas you used to be on fire for God, when you enter the the perceived 'neutral' zone your love for him grows cold—whether you like to admit it or not. You may be lukewarm at best, but that ironically is the worst place to be in, as we can see from Jesus' message to the church at Laodicea in ***Revelation 3:16 (NKJV), "because you are lukewarm, and neither cold nor hot, I will vomit you out of My mouth."***

We can see this false perception in the diagram. Figure 2 is the only one of the four scenarios that is impossible in reality.

Fig. 1 - Before Christ

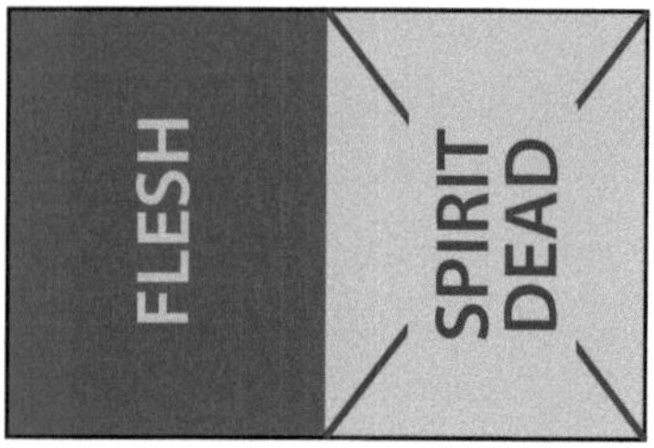

Fig. 2 - Christian's false perspective

Fig. 3 - Struggling Christian

Fig. 4 - Maturing Christian

Figure1 shows the state of our two natures before we were saved. Simply put, we only had one nature: the bad one. The selfish one. The carnal one. In this, by default, we displayed acts of the flesh; it may have been *good* flesh or *bad* flesh, but it was all flesh. In this state we were spiritually dead and therefore spiritually unaware. There was no conflict. We only had to think about our own desires and ambitions.

As mentioned, Figure 2 is the false perception that Christians can often get themselves, where they live most of their life in this *supposedly* neutral zone.

Figures 3 and 4 illustrate the true change at salvation. Our old nature is still in operation, but there's a new person in town—our new nature! Figure 3 shows a struggling Christian who is being led mainly by the flesh, whereas Figure 4 shows a growing Christian who is being led by the Spirit. This is where the battle can be seen.

Thankfully, all the odds of victory are stacked in our favour. Two spiritual truths are worth noting. Firstly, our new nature has the fullness of Christ living in it. One of the most explosive verses in the Bible—***Romans 8:11 (NIVUK)***—states, ***"And if the Spirit of God, who raised Jesus from the dead, lives in you."*** Secondly, the power the old nature had over you has been severed. ***Colossians 2:11 (AMP)*** says, ***"In Him you were also circumcised with a circumcision not made with hands, but by the [spiritual] circumcision of Christ in the stripping off of the body of the flesh [the sinful carnal nature]."*** You no longer *have* to do what you selfishly want to do.

So on the face of things it seems like a losing battle for the old nature. But not so fast with the assumptions! As we learned a couple of days ago, we still have a choice. God gave us free will to choose him. If we didn't express our love for him through choice, then that love would be robotic and void of any meaning. So we can choose to act according to the old *bad* nature or the new *good* nature. There's no *slightly* bad nature or *slightly* good nature.

Just as Jesus is our Lord and Master, so too the old nature is a master (side note: he's a defeated one). Therefore we choose to serve one or the other. ***Romans 6:16 (NLT)*** asks, ***"Don't you realize that you become the slave of whatever you choose to obey? You can be a slave to sin, which***

leads to death, or you can choose to obey God, which leads to righteous living." James 4:4 (NLT) puts another spin on the issue: ***"You adulterers! Don't you realize that friendship with the world makes you an enemy of God? I say it again: If you want to be a friend of the world, you make yourself an enemy of God."*** Pretty stark language.

So when we choose the old nature we become enemies of God! "But I thought I was saved?" you may exclaim. That may be the case, but unfortunately you can still *act* as an enemy. And you can do that by choosing just the littlest of sins. You see, it's not first and foremost about the *fruit* you display; it's about the *root* you choose. You're either serving one master or the other. There's no third-party involvement.

Finally, one example: let's say that you get drunk. That's clearly an act of the old nature as it isn't displaying any self-control (a fruit of the Spirit). Equally, you may just have one too many and get a bit tipsy. That *still* doesn't exercise self-control, so remains an act of the flesh. The margins may be different, but both outcomes are from the same ungoldly source.

QUESTIONS TO PONDER

- **Would you say that, generally speaking, you're moving more in the Spirit than in the flesh? If so, how would you evidence that?**
- **Are you, or have you ever been, 'lukewarm' as a Christian? If so, why? And what effect does it have on your relationship with God?**
- **Even though you're born again, do you accept that you still have a self-centred nature? If you do, how does it manifest most in your life?**

YESTERDAY'S SUMMARY: There's no neutral ground you can live in as a Christian; you're either walking in the flesh or in the Spirit.

DAY 19

PRIDE VS HUMILITY

LET'S START TODAY by talking about grace. Grace is not just what's commonly known as 'God's unmerited favour'. It's also God's power.

We were saved by grace in the first place, but we continually need grace to live out our faith in the ongoing pursuit of being saved. The Apostle Paul said in ***1 Corinthians 15:10 (AMP), "by the [remarkable] grace of God I am what I am, and His grace toward me was not without effect. In fact, I worked harder than all of the apostles, though it was not I, but the grace of God [His unmerited favor and blessing which was] with me."*** So grace is not just a means to salvation (often referred to as 'saving grace'), but it also empowers us to live the life of trust and obedience that we're called to (which is 'empowering grace').

2 Peter 3:18 (NLT) instructs us, ***"you must grow in the grace and knowledge of our Lord and Savior Jesus Christ."*** We grow in the grace of God through our increased understanding of his Word. This comes from spending time with him, reading the scriptures, meditating on them, and obeying them.

Now let's read ***James 4:6 (NLT), "God opposes the proud but gives grace to the humble."*** Add to that ***Matthew 23:12 (NIVUK): "those who exalt themselves will be humbled, and those who humble themselves will be exalted."*** We can see the two scriptures combined in today's graphic. It's not a complex illustration. That's why the devil loves to make it sound so obvious that we don't feel it needs spelling out or expanding on.

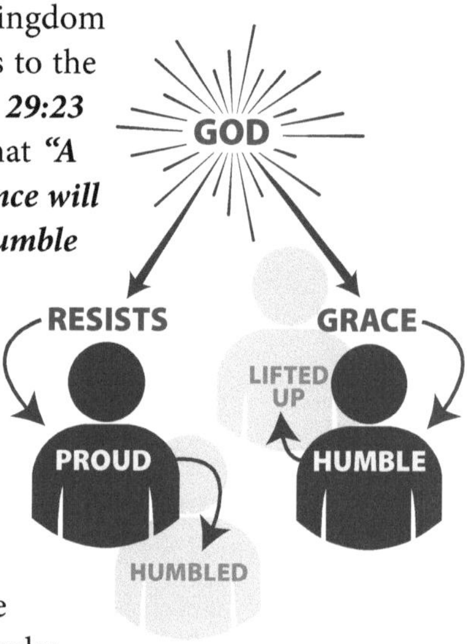

As with a lot of things in the Kingdom of God, they operate in opposite ways to the world's systems and values. ***Proverbs 29:23 (AMP)*** reiterates this by telling us that ***"A man's pride and sense of self-importance will bring him down, But he who has a humble spirit will obtain honor."*** Do you want to advance in the Kingdom of God? Do you want to be exalted by God? Do you want God to honour you? Humble yourself!

So what does humility look like in practice? You might think you've seen it in the church, but what you may have actually witnessed is *false* humility. Examples are: people deflecting praise that they deserve, an inability to take a compliment, the false portrayal of helplessness, self-deprecating humour, listening to others only to speak into their lives, and the admission of small sins to avoid bigger confessions—these are all signs of someone who is pretending to be humble.

Conversely, ***Proverbs 11:2 (AMP)*** gives us a good definition of what true humility is: "***When pride comes [boiling up with an arrogant attitude of self-importance], then come dishonor and shame, But with the humble [the teachable who have been chiseled by trial and who have learned***

to walk humbly with God] there is wisdom and soundness of mind."

To be humble is to be teachable. And that openness to learn from others brings about a remoulding of character, just like the clay on the potter's wheel. This whole process leads to wisdom and a sound mind—that's the fruit you can see come from a humble person.

Prophesying of the age that we live in today, ***Isaiah 57:15 (NLT)*** records God saying, ***"I live in the high and holy place with those whose spirits are contrite and humble. I restore the crushed spirit of the humble and revive the courage of those with repentant hearts."*** God is now living in the 'holy place' of our hearts because of the atoning work of Christ. But true, deep fellowship can only be had with the contrite and humble in heart. God sees through all false humility, and he cannot walk intimately with the disobedient. He's still with every believer—we're all still in communion with him—but only those who are acting in obedience to the Spirit and rejecting the demands of the fleshly nature are yoked to Jesus and walking in step with the Spirit. It's only here that the mysteries of God are unfolded and humility develops.

We've all got areas of our lives where pride can creep in, and for some it's taken up residence. Pride can masquerade as ministry ambition, godly authority and biblical understanding. Such things are repulsive to God. Pride is the believer's Kryptonite. It's the founding member of the fruit of the fleshly nature.

When Satan, then known as Lucifer, fell from his position in heaven, he hit the self-destruct button labelled 'pride'. He was high up in the angelic order, even to the point where he reflected God's glory back to God. As such many have described him as *heaven's worship leader*. But his downfall came when pride set in.

Isaiah 14:13-14 (NKJV) gives us five pride-filled 'I will' statements that ignited his downfall: ***"'<u>I will</u> ascend into heaven, <u>I will</u> exalt my throne above the stars of God; <u>I will</u> also sit on the mount of the congregation On the farthest sides of the north; <u>I will</u> ascend above the heights of the clouds, <u>I will</u> be like the Most High'"*** (emphasis mine).

Just as all sin is sin, all pride is pride. Don't be duped into thinking that your little bits of pride don't matter because you're not in Lucifer's league of colossal self-centredness.

PRIDE
LUCIFER
SIN

Pride is the genesis of all sin, so identifying it is crucial. Herein lies another problem. Just as we're so blinded from our own quirks and habits, we too can often be unaware of the manifestations of our selfish ambition without realising it.

A solution? Here are two: 1) Ask God to search your heart. ***Psalm 139:23-24 (MSG)*** says, ***"Investigate my life, O God, find out everything about me; Cross-examine and test me, get a clear picture of what I'm about; See for yourself whether I've done anything wrong."*** 2) Give permission to a mentor or trusted friend to speak into your life. ***Proverbs 27:6 (AMP)*** says, ***"Faithful are the wounds of a friend [who corrects out of love and concern], But the kisses of an enemy are deceitful [because they serve his hidden agenda]."*** Whichever you choose, do it regularly whilst you're still breathing.

QUESTIONS TO PONDER

- **Has God ever humbled you? What did it look like? How did you feel? What was the result?**
- **Have you ever felt exalted by God because you acted humbly? What happened, and how did you feel?**
- **If you don't have someone speaking into your life, why not? What's stopping you asking someone?**
- **If you do have a mentor or trusted friend that you meet with regularly, do you give them permission to call out any blind spots in you?**

YESTERDAY'S SUMMARY: All sin starts with pride. It's best to be humble rather than be humbled by God.

DAY 20 — GOOD WORKS

IT'S NOT ROCKET science to realise that bad practices come from the *old* nature and good works from the *new*. But we can so often be deceived by the devil into thinking that all 'good works' are born from our new, godly nature. I use the inverted commas on purpose, as not all good works are *God*-works.

Genuine, godly good works can only come from the realm of the new nature where Jesus is Master. It's really easy for us to do good works that haven't been issued by God. It just means that they've been signed off by ourselves, from the old self-centred nature.

The graphic overleaf shows how we naturally evaluate bad practices and good works by whether they seem worldly or godly. Yet actually the true test is not how they appear but who has authorised them.

Let me illustrate from a personal example. When I got the inspiration for writing this book, I was confident it was from God because concepts came that I couldn't have conjured up. Diagrams appeared in my mind. Revelation was downloading and words just flowed. I got all excited and without realising it (that's the key) started to trust in my own understanding. I was adding elements that weren't part of the original plan—so much so that I even changed the title. Long story short, this resulted in a whole week of research and writing which didn't make it into this book.

Here's the point: I was turning it into something that I thought was good. Notice the common factor in the shift: 'I'. *I* took over; *my* ideas, *my* thoughts. Things just ground to a halt as I realised that God was not authoring it any more; I was. Yes, it was good stuff that I was writing—I even learned new things in my research—but I wasn't being Spirit-led. I had to stop. I had to confess. I had to repent from walking according to the old nature instead of the new.

I could have fooled everyone into thinking it was *good work*, but the reality is that it was just *spiritualised* flesh.

This is illustrated very clearly in the scriptures. ***1 Corinthians 3:10-15 (NIVUK)*** says, ***"By the grace God has given me, I laid a foundation as a wise builder, and someone else is building on it. But each one should be built with care. For no one can lay any foundation other than the one already laid, which is Jesus Christ. If anyone builds on this foundation using gold, silver, costly stones, wood, hay or straw, their work will be shown for what it is, because the Day will bring it to light. It will be revealed with fire, and the fire will test the quality of each person's work. If what has been built survives, the builder will receive a reward. If it is burned up, the builder will suffer loss but yet will be saved - even though only as one escaping through the flames."***

What we do with our Christian lives is important. It doesn't determine our salvation—that was finalised at Calvary—but it does determine both our effectiveness in this life and our reward in the afterlife.

If Satan can get you to do good works from the old, self-centred nature, he can keep you preoccupied with minimal to no effectiveness in the Kingdom. No matter how theologically accurate my words were, or how well the sentences flowed, if I went with *my* ideas it would be nowhere near as effective as the ones you're reading now.

The fact is that *good* flesh is just as bad as *bad* flesh—they're both flesh! Having *good* ideas rather than *God* ideas can allow Satan to lead you astray, keeping you busy with uncommissioned work.

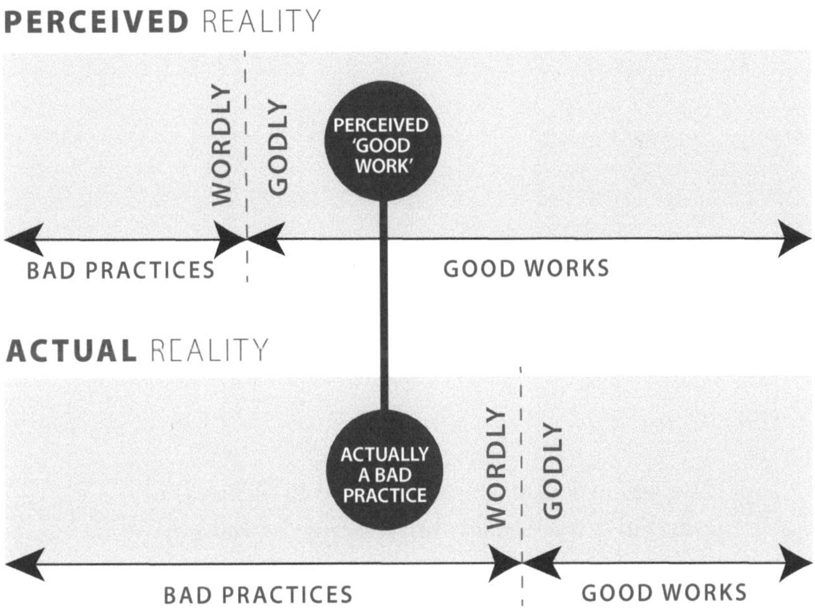

Take a moment right now to stop and think... The things you're doing for God right now, has God told you to do them? How would you know? We'll be expanding on these thoughts in our final section.

Walking with God is a continual learning experience. Whilst speaking about the building up of the body of Christ, the Apostle Paul says in ***Ephesians 4:13 (NLT), "This will continue until we all come to such***

unity in our faith and knowledge of God's Son that we will be mature in the Lord, measuring up to the full and complete standard of Christ."

Most Christians observe God from far away; that's why they don't always understand what he's doing. As you journey over the next few weeks, you'll get closer to God and will be more tuned in to his voice. You'll end up doing the things he asks, rather than assuming that you're doing his will.

QUESTIONS TO PONDER

- **Have you ever done a work for God *in the name of Jesus*, but it was actually orchestrated by *yourself*? What was it, and how did it go?**
- **How much do you depend on God to get you through a day, and how much do you rely on your own strength, ability and intellect? Reviewing today so far, what percentage would you apportion to both parties?**
- **How often do you ask God what good works for him he wants you to do? When was the last time you asked? And do you think you should consult him more?**

◀◀ **YESTERDAY'S SUMMARY:** Good works can be generated in the flesh. What looks good isn't always from God. If it isn't, it will account for nothing in the end.

DAY 21

EMPOWERED TO WIN

THE POWERS OF darkness want to play down the spiritual battle going on inside you. The more Satan can do that, the more he can keep you in the wilderness (that land of 'just enough'). But the truth is that there's a war raging inside you that's worthy of being made into a blockbusting Hollywood movie.

Even though 'war' doesn't sound like a good thing, this one is a war in which you have an arsenal of weapons—not just to fight with but to keep you in constant victory.

Ephesians 6:10-17 (NLT) is a classic text that lists the armour we need to fight this battle. ***"Be strong in the Lord and in his mighty power. Put on all of God's armor so that you will be able to stand firm against all strategies of the devil... put on every piece of God's armor so you will be able to resist the enemy in the time of evil. Then after the battle***

you will still be standing firm. Stand your ground, putting on the belt of truth and the body armor of God's righteousness. For shoes, put on the peace that comes from the Good News so that you will be fully prepared. In addition to all of these, hold up the shield of faith to stop the fiery arrows of the devil. Put on salvation as your helmet, and take the sword of the Spirit, which is the word of God."

It's beyond the scope of this book to delve into the area of spiritual warfare, but we definitely need to make some important points.

The first one is obvious, but a vital reminder: don't go into battle unarmed. You're no match for the devil in your own strength. He'll beat you up every time. But (a hugely significant *but*), when you go into battle in step with the Holy Spirit, you're invincible!

2 Peter 1:3 (NLT) says, **"By his divine power, God has given us everything we need for living a godly life."** *Everything.* We lack nothing as born-again believers; we just need to believe it and use the resources we've been given. We need to put on the armour of God each day, not leave it in our spiritual wardrobe.

Long-standing family friends of ours used to have a daily routine with their kids when they were younger: every day before school they'd go through the armour of God and spiritually dress themselves for the day ahead. Even as adults we should be more *childlike* in our faith and engage in similar, simple—yet ever so powerful—practices.

Let's now read the next verse from the Ephesians passage. ***Ephesians 6:18 (NLT): "Pray in the Spirit at all times and on every occasion."***

To be the overcomer and victor that God has called you to be is not just about walking in *step* with the Spirit; it's about walking in the *power* of the Spirit. As the verse above implies, you don't want to just pray in your own understanding (which is still good), you want to pray in the supernatural (which is even greater). And not just pray when you're in difficulty, but have a constant awareness of God where you can naturally engage in conversation at any given point of the day, no matter what you're doing, wherever you are.

For me, just speaking in tongues for a mere two minutes changes my whole being. Try it. It works! And there's no reason why it shouldn't, for ***1 Corinthians 14:4 (NLT)*** says, ***"A person who speaks in tongues is strengthened personally."***

Many people who move in charismatic church circles would claim that being filled with the Spirit gives you the power to witness. Their reference point is ***Acts 1:8 (NIVUK), "But you will receive power when the Holy Spirit comes on you; and you will be my witnesses in Jerusalem, and in all Judea and Samaria, and to the ends of the earth."*** Whilst this verse shows a direct link between being filled with the Spirit and receiving power to witness, it's just *one* empowerment.

Primarily, being filled with the Spirit empowers you to deny the flesh and obey God. ***James 4:6 (AMP)*** says, ***"He gives us more and more grace [through the power of the Holy Spirit to defy sin and live an obedient life that reflects both our faith and our gratitude for our salvation]."*** And ***Galatians 5:16 (NIVUK)*** instructs us to, ***"live by the Spirit, and you will not gratify the desires of the flesh."***

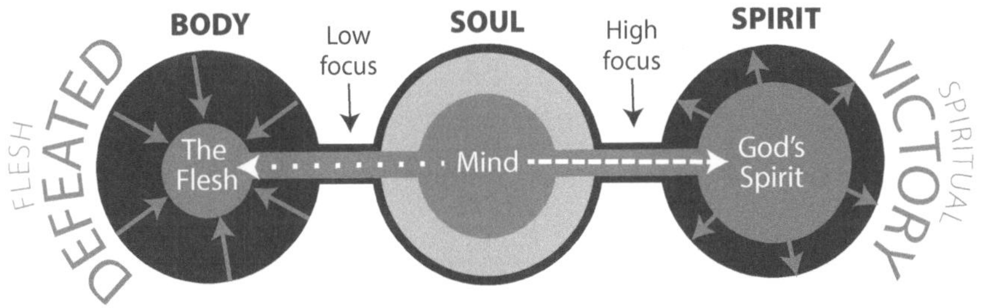

Once again, this isn't the time or the place to get into the theology of the baptism in the Holy Spirit, but boy, if you're not living in this realm then personally I can't see how you can get out of your wilderness into your Promised Land. Maybe you can. Maybe I have too much of a Pentecostal bias. But one thing's for sure: this way of living (being *filled* with the Spirit, not just *having* the Spirit) is what Jesus now gives us in his ascended position. Just before he went back into heaven, Jesus said in

Acts 1:5 (AMP), "For John baptized with water, but you will be baptized and empowered and united with the Holy Spirit, not long from now."

Have you ever asked for the gift of the Holy Spirit to come on you in power? If not, Jesus wants you to receive it. **Luke 11:13 (MSG)** says, **"don't you think the Father who conceived you in love will give the Holy Spirit when you ask him?"** Just as you received—in faith—the gift of eternal life, so too you can receive—in faith—the gift of the Holy Spirit. Have you done that before? If not, do it now. If you have, ask him to refill you. Ask every day. For **Ephesians 5:18 (AMP)** instructs us, **"be filled with the [Holy] Spirit and constantly guided by Him."** Just as you got saved and are *being saved*, so too you get filled with the Spirit, then have to be *being* filled, continually.

The devil will happily wait for you to have a spiritual *down day* before bringing his lies, deceits and temptations. Don't give him the opportunity. Live every moment in the power of the Spirit!

QUESTIONS TO PONDER

- **When was the last time you used a piece of spiritual armour? What was it? And what happened?**
- **Which piece of the armour of God do you use the most, and which do you use the least? Why do you think that is?**
- **If you speak in tongues for personal edification, in what ways can you begin exercising this more in your life?**
- **If you don't speak in tongues, why don't you ask God to fill you with his Spirit and, by faith, start speaking in your new heavenly language?**

WEEK 3 SUMMARY

Day 15: Carnal Living – Certain lifestyles within the Church are a bad advert for God. Christians need to understand they're living according to their old nature, and make a change.

Day 16: Choices, Choices – How you think determines the choices you make. The choices you make determine the actions you take.

Day 17: Personal Convictions – God convicts us of our sin when we first come to him. After that, he convicts us of what is right and wrong for us personally.

Day 18: Exposing Deception – There's no neutral ground you can live in as a Christian; you're either walking in the flesh or the Spirit.

Day 19: Pride vs Humility – All sin starts with pride. It's best to be humble rather than be humbled by God.

Day 20: Good Works – Good works can be generated in the flesh. What looks good isn't always from God. If it isn't, it will count for nothing in the end.

Day 21: Empowered to Win – God has supplied us with absolutely everything we need to gain daily victory in our lives. We just need to apply it.

We can flirt with sin,
but we'll never live in
harmony with it.

WEEK 4

Our barrier to intimacy: SIN

SIN 101

What is sin? I'd guess that a classic Christian response might be 'sin separates us from God'. Although that's true, it's not what it *is*; that's what it *does*. If you Googled the question for a few minutes you'd likely find these two definitions pop up frequently: 'breaking God's holy law' and 'missing the mark'.

I'm sure that when it comes to Christian living, you—like me—have missed the mark more times than you'd like to recall. Sin can often seem like it's got a grip on us, but we *can* peel back its fingers. It can at times feel overwhelming, but we can use this kind of experience as a catalyst for dealing with it. Just like Wet Wet Wet's 1990s record-selling cover song, *Love is all Around*, so is sin. It's everywhere. But we don't have to engage with it.

Now, as ***1 John 1:8 (NIVUK)*** says, ***"If we claim to be without sin, we deceive ourselves and the truth is not in us."*** And I'm sure you've asked yourself a question similar to the one in ***Proverbs 20:9 (NIVUK)***: ***"Who can say, 'I have kept my heart pure; I am clean and without sin'?"***

The ultimate consequence of sin is death. The Bible echoes this in ***Romans 6:23 (NIVUK)*** where it tells us that, ***"the wages of sin is death"***. This not only refers to physical death, but to the spiritual end: eternal separation from God.

The scriptures do bring us better news, however. In fact, it's the 'good news' that Jesus paid the price for our sin. ***Ephesians 1:7 (NLT)*** tells us that, ***"God is so rich in kindness and grace that he purchased our freedom with the blood of his Son and forgave our sin."*** When we believe in him for the forgiveness of our sins, then we are united with God, in Christ, forever.

Sin can be divided into three phases, just as we've seen with salvation. We're already saved—delivered from the *penalty* of sin; we're being saved—delivered from the *power* of sin; and will be saved in the future —delivered from the *presence* of sin.

Once again we find ourselves in the middle bit, focusing on the effect that sin has on our lives in the here and now.

SIN TODAY

Church history will always reveal a different emphasis within different ages or—more so in modern times—different generations. Some are minor, some major. Often we find an over-emphasis to counter an extreme. For instance, in the 1950s and '60s the church might have appeared somewhat over-the-top in its view of entertainment. Many older folk I looked up to when I first became a Christian would talk about how they weren't allowed to go dancing in clubs, or even go to the cinema. But nowadays low lighting, loud music and huge multimedia screens are very much the focus in some modern churches.

From the experience of my three decades being influenced by evangelicalism, I'd suggest that there's been a gradual 'playing down' of sin to where today it's often viewed fairly liberally. This is probably a rebound from extremes of legalism experienced in the decades prior.

Now, of course, churches and denominations will pitch their values with different priorities, so it's not just the church culture at various phases of time that changes certain emphasis. But whatever dictates the changes, it's important that we approach our doctrines and teachings from different perspectives, bringing a balanced approach that doesn't over-reach into the extremes.

PULL OUT THE STOPS

We saw in Week Two that there's a call to holiness on every Christian's life, but that's only going to be pursued by the elimination of sin in our lives. And sin is only forgiven when we confess it.

Satan loves it when sin isn't preached; he delights when brothers and sisters don't confront each other about it in love; he revels in the fact that the Church doesn't bring appropriate discipline when necessary; he knows full well that when believers start coming face to face with their sins 'all heaven can break loose'!

The devil is trying to destroy your spiritual life, whether you like it or not. He's trying to get you to operate in your own understanding. He wants you to think that confession doesn't really matter, and that repentance is not that necessary.

2 Peter 1:3 (NLT) tells us that, ***"By his divine power, God has given us everything we need for living a godly life"***. And ***Ephesians 1:3 (NLT)*** exclaims, ***"All praise to God, the Father of our Lord Jesus Christ, who has blessed us with every spiritual blessing in the heavenly realms because we are united with Christ."*** Basically, every born-again person is supercharged with the fullness of God, ready and able to take on the world—we just need to get that life out of us. Sin is the barrier that stops that from happening.

The barrier of sin can be like a glass ceiling for many. Because they don't know it's there, they just end up frustrated and disheartened when they don't see their prayers answered or they don't experience any great intimacy with God.

THE WEEK AHEAD

Last week we explored the opposition to our life of intimacy with God—the flesh. This week we're going to look into what gets in the way of our relationship with God—sin. The flesh pulls us away from God; sin separates us from his presence.

We'll be looking at what sin does to us—and also what it does to God. We'll be asking the Holy Spirit to reveal unknown sins in our lives that could be hindering our walk with him. We'll expose the basic time-tested—but still effective—strategies of Satan. We'll be investigating the necessary process that leads up to our sins being forgiven, as well as what we should do afterwards. And we'll be contrasting some of the sins of old found in the Bible with the sins we find in our lives today.

So as we cross over our halfway point of this six-week journey to greater intimacy with God, let's open our hearts to what he wants to reveal to us and teach us.

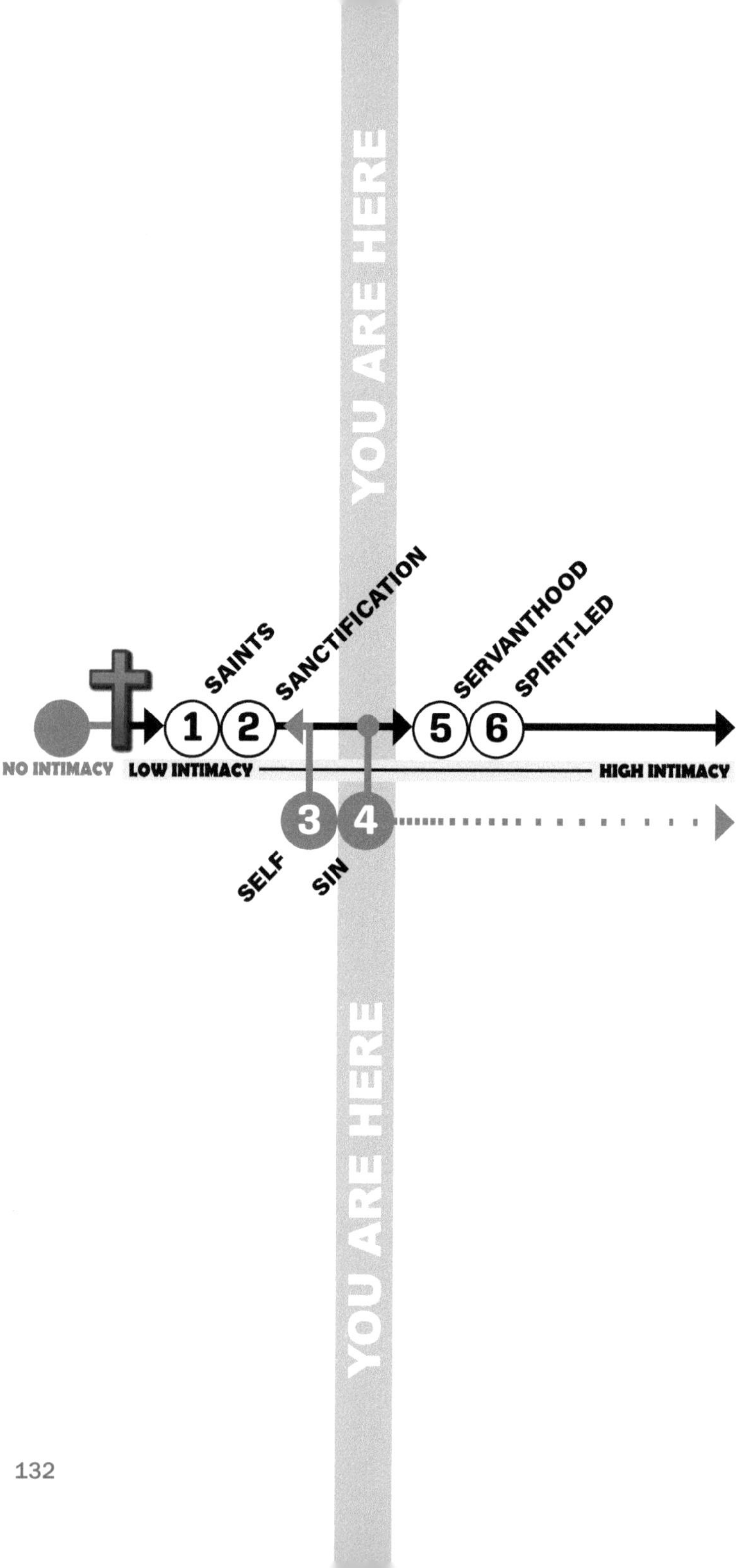
YOU ARE HERE
SAINTS
SANCTIFICATION
SERVANTHOOD
SPIRIT-LED
1
2
5
6
NO INTIMACY
LOW INTIMACY
HIGH INTIMACY
3
4
SELF
SIN
YOU ARE HERE

DAY 22

DISTANCED

ONE NIGHT ON a recent holiday I woke up at 4am from probably the most horrific dream I've ever had. It was a nightmare of sorts, in that I was confronted with the deep anguish and utter disappointment that sin causes.

In my dream I'd committed adultery. I can't remember the details (thank God), but just as bad, if not worse, was how I *felt* about the sin. Not only was the weight of it contributed by guilt, violation and trespass, but even more devastating was that the sin produced a distancing between God and me. It wasn't like a spiritual metaphor being played out in some kind of vision; it was like I was plunged into the depths of a spiritual reality at a level I didn't know existed.

The whole experience seemed so real that when I woke up I was confessing to every sin I could muster up.

God has spoken to me through dreams before, but this was different. One of the first scriptures that came to mind when I woke was ***Job 31:1 (NIVUK): "I made a covenant with my eyes not to look lustfully at a young woman."*** Then ***Matthew 5:27-28 (NIVUK)*** where Jesus said, ***"You have heard that it was said, 'You shall not commit adultery.' But I tell you that anyone who looks at a woman lustfully has already committed adultery with her in his heart."*** And then ***Ephesians 5:3 (NIVUK),*** where the Apostle Paul tells the church that among them, ***"there must not be even a hint of sexual immorality."*** No peeking. No glancing. Not even a fleeting fantasy.

If the weight of just one single sin was on me, how must Jesus have felt when he carried the burden of *every* sin, of *every* person, that had *ever* lived and was *going* to live? The nails in his body would have been one thing, the increasing suffocation another, but surely the real agony would have come from the sins of the world that he carried. And just a fraction of what I felt in being separated from God's presence was experienced fully by Jesus. It's no wonder that he cried out in ***Matthew 27:46 (NLT), "'Eli, Eli, lema sabachthani?' which means 'My God, my God, why have you abandoned me?'"*** Had God left his Son out to dry? Of course not! He was still relationally connected to the 'Son of *God*', but for the moments that he bore our sin God the Father had to turn away from the 'Son of *Man*', because a holy God can't be associated with any kind of impurity.

Thank God that the punishment for our sins has been paid, but there *are* spiritual consequences to unconfessed sins. Just as I felt in my dream, and as Jesus experienced on the cross, our sins can separate us from God's presence.

To more fully understand what happens when we sin, we need to know that there are three levels of God's presence we can experience:

1) OMNIPRESENCE – this is a 'universal' presence that everyone is a party to. ***Psalms 139:7 (NLT)*** says, ***"I can never escape from your Spirit! I can never get away from your presence!"***

2) INNER PRESENCE – this is God's 'known' presence living inside us through the Holy Spirit. ***1 Corinthians 3:16 (NKJV)*** asks, ***"Do you not***

know that you are the temple of God and that the Spirit of God dwells in you?"

3) MANIFEST PRESENCE – this is God's 'felt' presence communing with us. ***Exodus 33:15 (NIVUK)*** tells us, ***"Then Moses said to him, 'If your Presence does not go with us, do not send us up from here.'"***

Being free from the consequences of sin means that we can be united with God—just like the priests of old who entered the Holy Place of the Tabernacle. And now that we're ***royal priests (1 Peter 2:9)*** we have continuous access through the forgiveness of sins to the Most Holy Place, where we can enjoy intimate fellowship with him.

I used to think that I didn't need to repent of my sins after I was saved because Jesus had forgiven them—past, present *and future*. And that is true. But the next sin I commit will still have a spiritual consequence. Even the smallest of lies, even a momentary lustful thought, even a short temper exposed, will result in a form of separation from God. Not a separation from his love; that's impossible (***Romans 8:35***). Not a separation from his indwelling presence, for he's promised to be with us always (***Matthew 28:20***). But a separation from his holy manifest presence, where he shares the secrets of the Kingdom, where he imparts his blessings, and where we find courage and strength.

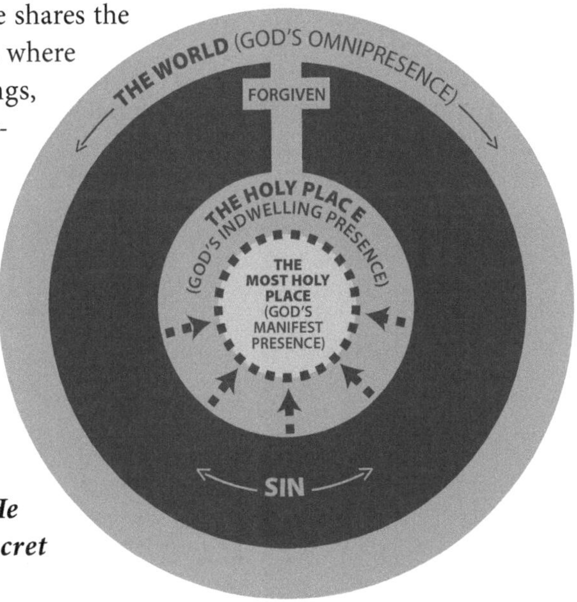

We should keep short accounts with God and confess our sins as they arise, so that we keep in close fellowship with him in the secret place of our hearts. ***Psalm 91:1 (NKJV)*** declares that ***"He who dwells in the secret***

place of the Most High shall abide under the shadow of the Almighty." Note that we aren't invited to *visit* God's presence at a church service or a prayer meeting; we're told that we can *dwell* in God's presence.

After my dream, I now read the following plea of King David with even more understanding and sympathy. And according to Jesus' words that we read a few moments ago, I guess that in my dream state I was no different to the king after he committed adultery with Bethsheba.

Psalm 51 (NLT) reads, ***"Have mercy on me, O God, because of your unfailing love. Because of your great compassion, blot out the stain of my sins. Wash me clean from my guilt. Purify me from my sin. For I recognize my rebellion; it haunts me day and night. Against you, and you alone, have I sinned; I have done what is evil in your sight. You will be proved right in what you say, and your judgment against me is just... Create in me a clean heart, O God. Renew a loyal spirit within me. Do not banish me from your presence, and don't take your Holy Spirit from me. Restore to me the joy of your salvation, and make me willing to obey you. Then I will teach your ways to rebels, and they will return to you."***

QUESTIONS TO PONDER

- When you have knowingly sinned, what does it feel like?
- When you know that you're not walking according to how God wants you to, how does that affect your relationship with him?
- Do you put up with sin in your life? How does that happen if you know it's wrong?
- When did you last feel the manifest presence of God in your life? What were you doing?

YESTERDAY'S SUMMARY: The penalty for our sins has been paid so that we can be 'in Christ', but the consequence of sinning is a distancing from God—that's why forgiveness each time is essential.

DAY 23

EXPOSING SINS

ONE DAY JESUS was with his disciples out in the community, telling some parables and doing a bit of teaching. During this time he was approached by a prominent young man.

We can pick up the account in ***Luke 18:18-24 (NKJV). 'Now a certain ruler asked Him, saying, "Good Teacher, what shall I do to inherit eternal life?" So Jesus said to him, "Why do you call Me good? No one is good but One, that is, God. You know the commandments: 'Do not commit adultery,' 'Do not murder,' 'Do not steal,' 'Do not bear false witness,' 'Honor your father and your mother.'" And he said, "All these things I have kept from my youth."'***

The commandments Jesus is referring to here are the Ten Commandments given to the people of Israel via Moses on the top of Mount Sinai. If you've ever studied the story, you'll know that God wrote on two tablets of stone. It's a common understanding that on one stone were four 'vertical' rules all about our relationship with *God*. On the other there were six 'horizontal' rules all about our relationship with *others*. The young man didn't think he had a *horizontal* problem: he proudly stated that he hadn't slept with anyone, he hadn't murdered anyone, he hadn't stolen from anyone and he hadn't lied to anyone.

The engagement continues: ***"So when Jesus heard these things, He said to him, 'You still lack one thing.'"*** (Let's pause there again for a second and note that Jesus has X-ray vision. So often in the scriptures we see that he knew the state of people's hearts.) Jesus didn't specifically tell him the sin, but it would have been obvious from his instruction. ***"Sell all that you have and distribute to the poor, and you will have treasure in heaven; and come, follow Me."*** Jesus revealed an internal issue of covetousness that the man wasn't aware of.

Just like the rich young ruler, we too have blind spots. *Overt* sins are visible, but *covert* sins are hidden (as illustrated by the first iceberg in the diagram below). Overt sins might look like anger, sarcasm, criticism, selfishness and envy. A lot of the time they are outward actions, but they could equally be internal issues like unbelief, for example. Covert sins are often attitudes, hidden away in the heart.

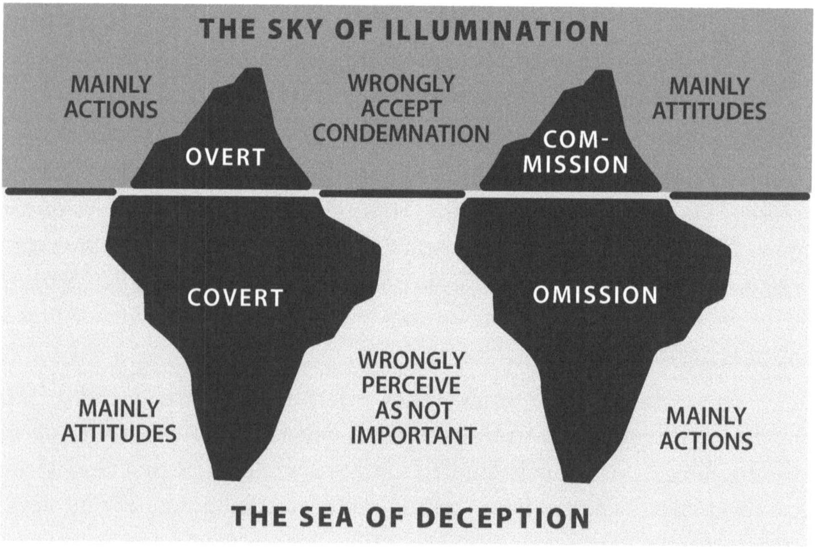

I'm super-competitive. It doesn't compute easily why people would want to play a game or sport simply for the fun of it and have no desire to win. Surely that's the main point of a game? (I know, I know, it's the taking part as well.) Kate is not competitive. Not one bit. After 30 years of marriage I've come to terms with that as best I can. She's not into games as much as me, but very recently—being the model Christian she is—she said to me, 'Do you fancy a game of Scrabble?' Where did that come from? She doesn't like word games and she hardly ever wins at them! Anyway, battle commenced (on my part, anyway). Ladies first. J-O-I-S-T-E-R. Fifteen points for the word itself; on the centre double-word score making it 30 points; an extra 50 points for getting all her letters out. Eighty points in total! This was unprecedented. With *my* opener I can only manage a measly seven points. Kate's go again: D-E-N-S. Doesn't sound so bad on first reading, but she's put her 'S' on the end of JOISTER to make JOISTERS and both words are on a triple word score again. Another 60 points for her tally. I can only muster a score of 10 with my next move. Then to rub it in further Kate's scores 27 next, with F-A-I-T-H.

Why am I telling you this? Because something rose up inside me that I didn't know was there. I was increasingly becoming agitated and frustrated because my chances of winning were waning—and I couldn't do anything about it. It was a covert sin. Something that I didn't know was there. God set me up that afternoon. Kate won. My sins were exposed. And confessed. And repented of. Finally, a win for me!

Let's briefly look at the other iceberg. Sins of *commission* are things we do wrong. Many times they're attitudes like jealousy, pride, covetousness and apathy. We know we shouldn't do them, which makes it harder when they come and slap us in the spiritual face. As Paul says in ***Romans 7:19 (NIVUK), "I do not do the good I want to do, but the evil I do not want to do".*** But sins of *omission* are things we know we should do, but don't do. That may sound harsh, but it's true. ***James 4:17 (NLT)*** says, ***"it is sin to know what you ought to do and then not do it."*** Note that you've got to have *knowledge* of the good you should do. When we were baby Christians, fresh out of the spiritual womb, we didn't know what God's standards were so we couldn't be accountable for them. But as we read our Bibles we started to understand more about the ways of God, and the challenges and choices then started to flow.

Maybe you know it's good to fellowship, but you skip church because you feel a bit tired. Maybe you've felt convicted in your heart to give financially, but let the offering bowl pass you by. Perhaps your neighbour is vulnerable right now, but you don't reach out to them. Maybe God is challenging you to get involved in a specific ministry, but you have a whole list of 'valid' excuses that have stopped you from engaging. Every moment you delay obeying God, you're in sin. These words may be hurting right now, but sometimes the truth hurts. Don't shoot the messenger.

Yes, sin is atoned for. Your eternal salvation is secure (even if you're committing sins you're unaware of). But all the while known sin is unconfessed, you're preventing yourself from having precious fellowship with God. Even with Christ's indwelling presence it can feel a lonely place when you know you're missing out on the fullness of God. At such a point, the devil will throw condemnation your way to make you feel worse. Meanwhile God is longing for you to come and humbly approach him. The Holy Spirit is compelled to help us in such a time of need. And Jesus sympathises with our weakness. When sins are confessed, God closes in on us with forgiveness and beckons us towards repentance—all so that we can enjoy him and his presence.

QUESTIONS TO PONDER

- **In what ways can you identify unknown (covert) sins in your life?**
- **When was the last time you were confronted by sin that you didn't realise was there? What was it, and have you repented of it?**
- **What things do you know you should be doing, but either haven't got round to yet or have devalued?**

YESTERDAY'S SUMMARY: The devil wants to blind us to our sins, because he knows they separate us from intimacy with God, reduce our effectiveness and weaken our witness.

DAY 24

SCAMMED

WE'VE PROBABLY ALL encountered them one way or another—whether you've won a prize and just need to pay for shipping, you're offered goods in an online flash sale, or you're told to give a password because your account has been compromised—scamming is a lucrative business for criminals.

The success that fraudsters have is mainly down to deceiving you into thinking something is true when it's not. It's a trick that's been around since the beginning of time. Let's read ***Genesis 3:1-7 (AMP): "Now the serpent was more crafty (subtle, skilled in deceit) than any living creature of the field which the Lord God had made. And the serpent (Satan) said to the woman, "Can it really be that God has said, 'You shall not eat from any tree of the garden'?" And the woman said to the serpent, "We may eat fruit from the trees of the garden, except the fruit from the***

tree which is in the middle of the garden. God said, 'You shall not eat from it nor touch it, otherwise you will die.'" But the serpent said to the woman, "You certainly will not die! For God knows that on the day you eat from it your eyes will be opened [that is, you will have greater awareness], and you will be like God, knowing [the difference between] good and evil." And when the woman saw that the tree was good for food, and that it was delightful to look at, and a tree to be desired in order to make one wise and insightful, she took some of its fruit and ate it; and she also gave some to her husband with her, and he ate."

It all starts with identity. Like the scammer pretending to email you from your bank—with a genuine-looking logo and familiar signature panel—so too Satan comes in the disguise of a snake. (This may sound weird to us today, but everything was new for Eve so it's fairly safe to suggest that she just thought this must have been the norm.)

Next comes the twisting of the truth. Like the bank scammers may tell you that your account has been hacked—making it sound highly plausible—Satan in the garden deviates from the truth by saying, ***"Can it really be that God has said, 'You shall not eat from any tree of the garden'?"*** He's switching the narrative to get her to think that God is forbidding them *all* trees, but in fact it was just *one*.

Then comes the lie wrapped in deception. 'Your account has been compromised! Log in and update your information,' the scammer instructs. For Eve, it was the lie that she won't *really* die; God just doesn't want her to have the same knowledge that *he* has. Eve let that seed of doubt enter her head and continued to nurture it: 'But surely being a bit more like God can't be a bad thing? Maybe we could actually help God with this extra knowledge?'

The final escalation comes when the lust of the eyes is engaged and the gratification of the heart is considered. ***"When the woman saw that the tree was good for***

food, and that it was delightful to look at, and a tree to be desired..." Crunch! Sin was conceived. The Cosmos shivered. Everything changed. Through Adam and Eve's disobedience their relationship with God was never the same. Only through Jesus Christ was it restored, but that rescue plan was thousands of years away.

This snake mentioned in the first book of the Bible is also in the last book. ***Revelation 12:9 (AMP)*** tells us again about this ***"age-old serpent who is called the devil and Satan, he who continually deceives and seduces the entire inhabited world"***. Satan may be defeated through the finished work of Christ, but he's still up to his old tricks of scamming God's children. He's constantly trying to minimise the effectiveness of every blood-bought, born-again person on the planet.

James 1:14-15 (NIVUK) spells out exactly how it happens, and it's no different to what he did in the garden: ***"but each person is tempted when they are dragged away by their own evil desire and enticed. Then, after desire has conceived, it gives birth to sin; and sin, when it is full-grown, gives birth to death."***

Satan is the one who tempts us, but it's our fleshly 'evil desires' that do all the hard work leading up to sin. Temptation merely ignites the desires of the flesh. So Satan's temptations aren't actually that great. It's our flesh engaging our soul that lures us into disobeying God. It works something like the process of engaging with a slide:

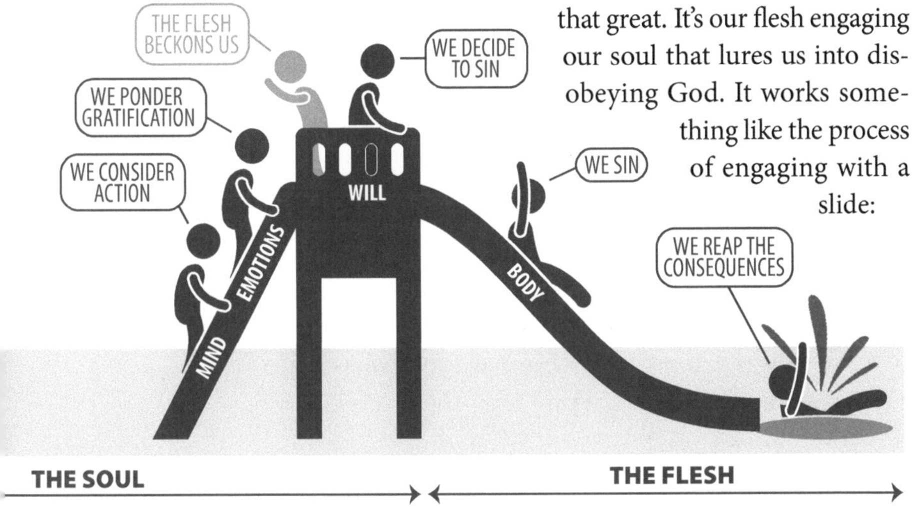

THE MIND: We are dragged away, tempted by our own carnal desires. We see the bait, but not the hook. **THE EMOTION:** Once the carnal mind has engaged the possibility of 'play time' it's then enticed by the wickedness of the heart. We move from thinking about the sin to feeling its gratification. **THE WILL:** The final step toward sin is positioning ourselves to engage. From here it's hard—but not impossible—to resist, as we are only one movement away from an ungodly adrenaline rush. **ACTIONS:** The birth of sin is when we fully let go in our spirit and let the flesh call the shots. The flesh loves it, but it doesn't take long for the pleasures of sin to subside, leaving us to reap the consequences. **DEATH:** By God's grace and mercy he has delivered us from ultimate death. The unsaved will end up spiritually dead, but in Christ we are given life. However, although we can be cleaned up again through forgiveness, if we don't truly repent our hearts become hardened and we end up living something like we did before we found Jesus.

Hebrews 3:12-13 (NIVUK) tells us, ***"See to it, brothers and sisters, that none of you has a sinful, unbelieving heart that turns away from the living God. But encourage one another daily, as long as it is called 'Today', so that none of you may be hardened by sin's deceitfulness."***

QUESTIONS TO PONDER

- **Can you look back to a time where you can see now that the devil scammed you by leading you into sin? What happened?**
- **Examining your spiritual walk and relationship with God right now, where do you see yourself in the diagram on the previous page? Are you being directed by the Spirit in all areas, or have you fallen into a stage of temptation somewhere?**

YESTERDAY'S SUMMARY: Satan uses the same old tricks to scam us into sin; once we fall for his lies and deceit an ungodly chain reaction can so easily kick in.

DAY 25

GRIEVING & PLEASING

WE ARE CREATED in the image of God, so if we display emotions then it figures that we probably get them from God. Like Father, like son (or daughter). We can see this from the scriptures. For instance, God gets angry with all unrighteousness (Romans 1:18); he shows compassion to his people (Psalm 135:14); he gets jealous (Exodus 34:14); and of course he displays a supreme love for the world (John 3:16).

Jesus had emotions too. Again, not surprising as he's the Son of God. ***Colossians 1:15 (NLT)*** tells us, that ***"Christ is the visible image of the invisible God."*** Recall some of his emotions yourself—the time he wept over Jerusalem (***Luke 19:41***); the zeal for his house when he upturned the tables of the money-lenders in the temple (***John 2:15***); his frustration with his disciples because they couldn't cast a demon out of a boy (***Luke 9:41***).

But for today we're going to expose a couple of specific emotions.

Firstly: Grief. After God finished his outstanding work of creation, we unfortunately don't have to turn that many pages of the Bible to discover that it all went terribly wrong. As a result of the fall humans had become wicked—so much so that God became deeply troubled. Troubled to the extent of sending a flood on the earth so he could start again with a faithful few people (Noah and his family) who were saved in an ark. Leading up to this point it got so bad that ***Genesis 6:6 (NKJV)*** says, ***"the Lord was sorry that He had made man on the earth, and He was grieved in His heart."***

We can see that same kind of sorrow and upset hundreds of years later when God delivered his people (Israel) out of slavery. They hadn't long been miraculously set free before they started moaning and grumbling. They were an ungrateful, often rebellious, people. ***Psalm 95:10 (NKJV)*** records God saying: ***"For forty years I was grieved with that generation, And said, 'It is a people who go astray in their hearts, And they do not know My ways.'"*** You and I might have a bad day at the office or possibly even a season of sadness for some particular reason, but God was grieving for a whole generation!

Finally, fast forward to the New Testament—***Ephesians 4:30-31 (NIVUK),*** which says, ***"do not grieve the Holy Spirit of God, with whom you were sealed for the day of redemption. Get rid of all bitterness, rage and anger, brawling and slander, along with every form of malice."*** Even today we can cause God grief and sorrow by our actions.

Let's understand something important before we continue: God is not a victim of his emotions. Yes, he has feelings, but he's not dictated to by them—he sees the end from the beginning. He knows they're coming, but he engages with them on another level. You see, God can have two different perspectives on a single situation. He looks at our sin through a narrow lens and is grieved, but at the same time he can widen that lens and, in his wisdom, see our sin as a thread that's woven into a bigger plan that he has in mind for us.

Think about Joseph in the Old Testament when he was betrayed by his brothers. They sold him into slavery. But decades later, by the grace of

God and his faithfulness, Joseph was promoted to second in command over the whole nation of Egypt. During his prosperous tenure God had him interpret a dream about a famine. Long story short, he stockpiled grain before the hard times hit. When the famine struck, his brothers came from Canaan to buy food. The conclusion of the long-standing family saga seems to come in ***Genesis 50:20 (NIVUK)*** where Joseph says, ***"You intended to harm me, but God intended it for good to accomplish what is now being done, the saving of many lives."*** God saw the sin of the brothers through the narrow lens, but could also see the same event through the wide lens, using it for a bigger purpose. God doesn't always act as justly as we would want him to at the time, but we have to trust that he sees the end from the beginning and often has higher purposes in mind.

So we can grieve God, but the Bible is clear that we can also elicit another emotion from God: pleasure.

How does this happen? How can we bring pleasure to him instead of bringing grief? Well, let's start with ***Hebrews 11:6 (NIVUK): "without faith it is impossible to please God, because anyone who comes to him must believe that he exists and that he rewards those who earnestly seek him."*** To start pleasing God you need to believe in him, and believe that he blesses everyone who pursues him.

So how do we get the faith needed to please him? ***Romans 10:17 (NKJV)*** tells us that, ***"faith comes by hearing, and hearing by the word of God."*** So the more we absorb his Word—like our personal daily reading of the Bible and meditation of

scripture, listening to sermons, and studying the Bible—the more faith we will build up. And, in turn, the more we will please God. There's no middle ground where God is just stuck in a neutral emotional gear when it comes to our relationship with him; we're either grieving him by acting according to the flesh, or pleasing him by walking in the Spirit.

We also need to remember in it all that ***James 2:26 (NKJV)*** says, ***"faith without works is dead."*** So we need to put our faith into action by being obedient to the words God speaks to us. For example, ***Hebrews 12:1-2 (NIVUK)*** instructs us to ***"throw off everything that hinders and the sin that so easily entangles, and to run with perseverance the race marked out for us, fixing our eyes on Jesus, the pioneer and perfecter of faith."***

In short, this is what we need to do to stop grieving God and start pleasing him: stop sinning and faithfully serve the Lord from a place of commitment to his Word. Even shorter: walk in the Spirit, not your flesh.

QUESTIONS TO PONDER

- **If you and God swapped places, how would you feel when your children sinned? How would their sorrow and confession change things?**
- **Why is it important to review how much you have sinned and how much you have acted in faith?**
- **If faith pleases God so much, why don't we exercise it more often?**
- **What one thing could you exercise faith in that would accomplish something positive in the Kingdom? Do you think it would please God if you did?**

◀◀ **YESTERDAY'S SUMMARY:** As his children we can make our Father God both happy and sad, through faith and sin respectively.

DAY 26 — THE REFINING PROCESS

DURING WEEK TWO we looked at sanctification and how God calls us to become more and more holy. This is mainly achieved by the elimination of sin from our lives.

Let's go to the prophet Jeremiah to see how this works in practice. In the first 45 chapters of the book God speaks of a discipline coming to the nation of Israel; then in the remaining chapters he deals with the surrounding nations—Moab is one of them. Let's read ***Jeremiah 48:11 (NKJV): "Moab has been at ease from his youth; He has settled on his dregs, And has not been emptied from vessel to vessel, Nor has he gone into captivity. Therefore his taste remained in him, And his scent has not changed."***

The prophet here is using a wine-making analogy to communicate his message. Back in Jeremiah's day they would tread or press the grapes and put the juice into a vessel. Yeast would then be added, creating a chemical reaction with the fruit's natural sugars to produce the alcohol. This is the fermentation process which takes a few weeks. But there's something else happening during this time, something that will ultimately create a clean, pure, pleasurable wine.

During this phase dregs settle at the bottom: pips, skin, stalks and any impurities that may have found their way in became sediment that separated from the purity of the juice. At the right time, the wine-makers would pour off the contents into another, clean vessel, being careful not to transfer any of the dregs at the end. The process would be repeated several times so that the finished product would be as pure as possible.

Through this illustration God is saying to Moab that there are sins they've committed that haven't been dealt with. They've been complacent; they've not changed for the better; they've just carried on like nothing is wrong; they've rested on their sinful laurels. They've sat on their 'dregs'.

We can still use this analogy in our lives today. Throughout the course of your walk with God you'll be able to identify specific times where you felt like you were 'poured out'. There was a disturbance in your life; a test or trial that brought with it challenges; a change that was difficult. There's a fair chance that you're in one of these *pourings* now.

After I'd been a Christian for about four years, I remember a significant pouring. God clearly spoke to my heart about changing my place of work. I was enjoying my first ever job of real value, doing something I was good at. I had a good salary and my first company car. But after a few years I was headhunted by my old boss. It looked like career suicide on paper, but I just *knew* that God was calling me. My current boss desperately didn't want me to leave; after an hour of him trying to change my mind I had to play my trump card and tell him that God had told me to go. At this point—not understanding the nature of obeying God—he asked me to name my own salary. After repeating my mantra stating allegiance to God's instruction, he finally gave up and wished me all the best.

Now you'd think that this would be a great testimony ending in God's goodness and blessing, but actually at times during the next three years it

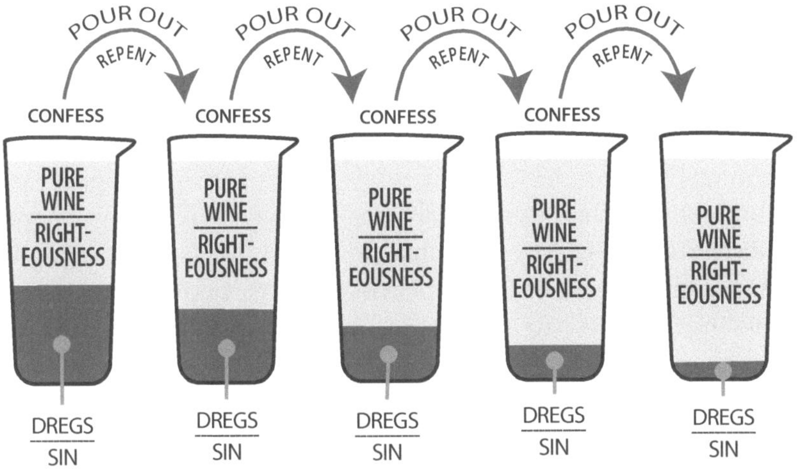

was littered with disappointment, frustration and anxiety. I thought it was just a part of 'suffering for Christ' at the time and maybe about learning to be a bit more patient. That could have been part of it, but looking back now I can see that God was identifying impurities in my life.

Unfortunately, I didn't realise that he was teaching me—in this instance, to honour my employer. I didn't have a terrible attitude towards him, but at times I didn't have a respectful one either! This was far more important to God than it was to me. Unfortunately I didn't even know that lesson was happening. I had 'settled on my dregs', focusing on the obedience of moving jobs but not understanding the sin that God was trying to get rid of.

There have been many other instances I could cite. I'm sure you can too. They may involve a career, a relationship, your health or your finances. Equally they may be seemingly smaller outpourings such as a disappointment, a word spoken out of turn, a false accusation or waiting on a promise from God. He's not so much interested in what they are, but that we *identify* them and *deal* with them.

God's not going to be pleased if, like Moab, we're resting on sin in our lives that has been there for a while. As the verses say, we can end up with a bitter taste in our mouths and a stench of staleness that can put people off wanting to associate with us.

If you think about it now, you can probably bring to mind people in your church who you'd rather not be around because they give off a 'worldly' aura. It may be that they stink of sarcasm, negativity or complaining. Or it may be the more subtle smell of arrogance, pride and unforgiveness. Whatever the stench, the chances are (like me with levels of disrespect for my new boss) that God is waiting for them to see the dregs of sin in their lives and repent of them. We don't want to be that person without realising it.

The way forward is to examine our hearts. Do a fruit check—regularly. Are you responding with the fruit of the Spirit or with the fruit of the flesh? It's going to be one or the other. If it's the stinking, bitter-tasting flesh, then this is your opportunity to confess it and repent from it.

Don't delay. Don't settle in your sin. Deal with it and keep in close companionship with the lover of your soul.

QUESTIONS TO PONDER

- **In what ways have you felt God 'pouring you out' of one situation to another?**
- **Though it may have been an opportunity for the devil to cause havoc in your life, can you recall a situation where God worked good through it? In what ways did you become more Christ-like as a result?**
- **Are you going through some trial or temptation right now? If so, and you had to guess, what do you think is the biggest lesson that God is trying to teach you?**

YESTERDAY'S SUMMARY: Our pursuit of holiness is achieved by constantly identifying and eliminating sin in our lives.

DAY 27

IDOLATRY

GOD'S PLAN TO rescue his people from slavery in Egypt around 1,300 BC was littered with powerful acts that you'd probably only see in a Marvel film. Our true superhero Yahweh sent 10 plagues on Israel's enemies; he sent an angel of death throughout the Egyptian community; he parted the Red Sea so that around two to three million people could walk across a dry sea-bed; and he closed the waters behind them, wiping out Pharaoh's chasing army.

God then took the Israelites to Mount Sinai. He was at the top of the mountain, and Moses was called up to receive the Ten Commandments. He was having a *summit* with God at the *summit* of the mountain. In ***Exodus 32*** we see the redeemed nation of Israel waiting for Moses to come back down; but after 40 days they thought he'd abandoned them, so they built a golden calf to worship instead. God was furious! And quite rightly so. He'd only just performed all those miracles in their sight and, before you know it, they were turning to images *of* God rather than God *himself.* Such is the vulnerability of the human heart.

The great irony in this account is that, whilst Moses was receiving the commandments from God at the top of the mountain, the Israelites started breaking them at the bottom of the mountain. ***Exodus 20:3 (NLT)*** gives us God's first commandment: ***"You must not have any other god but me."*** Moses was preparing to spiritually marry God to his people through a covenant relationship, but before anyone could say 'I do' the nation of Israel had seemingly prostituted herself to another god!

Aaron—deputy leader at the time—took all the gold earrings off the people that they had plundered from the Egyptians, and melted them down into an image of a calf. Now let's not get too hard on the instigators here; after all, they declared in ***Exodus 32:4 (NKJV), "This is your god, O Israel, that brought you out of the land of Egypt!"*** They recognised God's mighty power, but they mixed it with the pagan practices of Egypt where they worshipped many different gods in the form of crafted objects. So in fact it was more like the second command that they were breaking, not the first. That says, in ***Exodus 20:4,5 (NLT), "You must not make for yourself an idol of any kind or an image of anything in the heavens or on the earth or in the sea. You must not bow down to them or worship them, for I, the Lord your God, am a jealous God who will not tolerate your affection for any other god."***

We might think such an ancient story has no relevance to 21st century Christian living, particularly in the developed western world; but if we stop and think we can see the exact same things happening, just under different guises.

As believers we've experienced God's power firsthand in our lives. Many a different story can be told but they all carry the same theme, just like the Israelites' experience, of God rescuing us from slavery into freedom. Your freedom might have been from hopelessness, loneliness, loss, hurt, addiction or fear—whatever it was, God delivered you by his might and brought you to himself.

However, like Israel, we too can quickly compromise our relationship with God by mixing in worldly lifestyles. Before we know it, we can be subscribing to a form of progressive Christianity that devalues scripture, promotes collective salvation, or prescribes a social justice gospel. Or you might get lured into a 'prosperity gospel' where God's goodness is measured in the possessions we own and the wealth we have amassed.

Idolatry comes in many shapes and sizes. Your god or idol might not be the security of money in the bank, the house you live in or the car you drive; it could be the music you listen to, the sports team you follow or the knowledge you have acquired. It could involve fitness, food, a career or a relationship. It could even be a ministry or a spiritual gift. Again, these can all be blessings in their own rights, but they can also be idols in our lives—even as God-loving, Bible-believing Christians.

But how can we tell? What's the acid test? Well, if God asked you to give any one of them up, would you be able to? Of course we'd like to unequivocally give the Christian answer *yes*, but I'm asking you privately, with no one else but God listening. Could you? Really? Without hesitation? If not, then it's time to take it to God.

A simple way to keep yourself from the entrapment of idolatry is to worship God for *who he is*, not *what he gives*. We should be thankful for all the blessings he supplies, but we worship the *provider*, not the *provision*.

When our focus is fixed on the *creation* rather than the *Creator*, we give power and prominence to those things. This is very subtle. We don't realise it's happening, but our grip on our idols tightens, turn on turn, the more we inadvertently worship them. That's why it's vital to take regular stock of our lives as to what really matters to us. If we are vulnerable enough to allow God to search our hearts and identify such areas in our lives, it can be one of the most liberating and empowering experiences. When idolatry is brought into the light and we turn away from it, Satan loses all power in that particular area and God's empowering grace can flow directly through us once again.

With Jesus' help you can identify and dethrone any idols, establishing your loyalty to him once more as Lord alone. We'll look into the practicality of doing this tomorrow.

Let me quickly bring one final watch-out that'll be applicable to some. It's about the sin of self-sufficiency. Many gifted people in the body of Christ are prone to fall into this evil practice to differing degrees. I certainly have. ***Jeremiah 2:13 (NIVUK)*** says, ***"My people have committed two sins: They have forsaken me, the spring of living water, and have dug their own cisterns, broken cisterns that cannot hold water."***

Even as God-fearing people, when we do the works of God in our own strength, according to our own plans, with our own agenda, then not only do we displease him (for it's impossible to please him without faith), but we take all the potential glory away from him. Furthermore, our efforts end up looking like cheap imitations of what God had originally planned and purposed. This is why prayer is vital in our lives. Prayers for his strategies, prayers for his strength and prayers for his timing.

QUESTIONS TO PONDER

- **Like Abraham was told to give up his child and the rich young ruler was told to give up his money, if God told you to give up something precious to you, would you? Could you, for example, sacrifice a relationship, a job, a career, a ministry, a car, a house or your time?**
- **What are the top three things that God has blessed you with in your life? Have you ever idolised them—that is, have they ever got in the way of your intimacy with God?**
- **If you had one pleasure in life that came anywhere near to the pleasure that God offers us, what would it be?**

YESTERDAY'S SUMMARY: Idolatry can be alive and well today inside followers of Christ. Without realising it, we can be worshipping the provisions of God above the person of God.

DAY 28

GETTING RID

WE'RE GOING TO conclude our focus on sin this week by going through the flow chart overleaf. There are various important words we need to be clear about in order to understand the essential process of getting rid of the effects of sin in our lives. Some words sound similar, but they are in fact distinctly different.

We've learned several things about sin the last few days, not least that it all comes from the root of pride. We also know that the penalty for our sins has been paid, but we still need forgiveness from God to maintain a close relationship with him in the Most Holy Place, where his manifest presence is felt.

So whenever we sin, it's important that we first and foremost recognise it (remember, it might be something covert that God is bringing to the surface). Search your heart. Regularly. Even daily. You clean your body and your teeth on a daily basis, so why wouldn't you clean your soul?

When we miss the mark by sinning, God is ready to correct our aim. Correction may come from the scriptures, possibly from reading the scriptures or listening to a sermon; it may come from a rebuke directly from the Holy Spirit; it may come from a spiritual authority or a mentor. Whichever way it arrives at your door, it's God's discipline being delivered in love. As ***Hebrews 12:5-6 (NLT)*** says, ***"have you forgotten the encouraging words God spoke to you as his children? He said, 'My child, don't make light of the Lord's discipline, and don't give up when he corrects you. For the Lord disciplines those he loves, and he punishes each one he accepts as his child.'"*** If you feel the discipline of God in your life, that is further confirmation that you're his child and that he wants the best for you!

After correction comes conviction. The Holy Spirit came into the world to convict it of sin. Jesus says in ***John 16:8 (NLT)*** that ***"when he comes, he will convict the world of its sin, and of God's righteousness, and of the coming judgment."*** Although we've already been convicted of our sin in the general sense, there's still an inner conviction that we have regarding what we believe is right and wrong. That may differ slightly from person to person.

When that conviction sets in, it triggers sorrow. Now we have to be careful at this point because sorrow can be a case of mistaken identity. There are two types of sorrow: 'worldly' and 'godly'. They look almost identical to the innocent bystander, but upon closer examination they're very different indeed.

Worldly sorrow exhibits only sorrow around getting caught. It propels you back into the realm of pride, where the devil will do his best to condemn you. He wants to make you feel punished for what you've done, as if it was some kind of penance. Then, because there's been no genuine sorrow, you're left not only out of sorts with God but in a vulnerable position where you can so easily be tempted again to follow the same path of sin. If he can get us to keep repeating the same action, and thinking that our worldly sorrow has dealt with the situation, we'll form a habitual sin

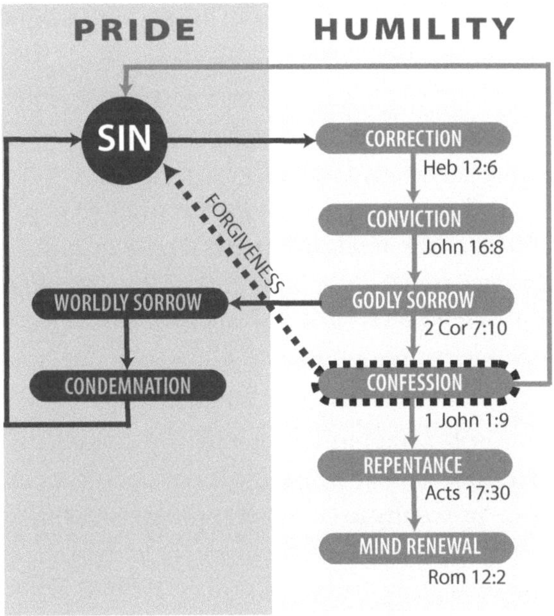

that eventually could be an entry point for the demonic.

But when we instead stay humble before God and exhibit godly sorrow, then we are led away from sin. ***2 Corinthians 7:10 (NLT)*** says, ***"For the kind of sorrow God wants us to experience leads us away from sin and results in salvation. There's no regret for that kind of sorrow. But worldly sorrow, which lacks repentance, results in spiritual death."***

Worldly sorrow doesn't lead to repentance; godly sorrow does. But the last stop before we arrive there is confession. ***1 John 1:8-9 (NLT)*** points out, ***"If we claim we have no sin, we are only fooling ourselves and not living in the truth. But if we confess our sins to him, he is faithful and just to forgive us our sins and to cleanse us from all wickedness."*** To confess is to 'speak out'. It can be done privately to God or, as we see in ***James 5:16 (NLT),*** it can be done to another person or group of people: ***"Confess your sins to each other and pray for each other so that you may be healed."***

Confession brings about the spiritual cleansing that we need whilst we are 'being' saved. It activates the all-important forgiveness of sins, but also leads us to repentance. ***Acts 17:30 (NLT)*** says, ***"God overlooked people's ignorance about these things in earlier times, but now he commands everyone everywhere to repent of their sins and turn to him."*** Although we repented from our sins in the general sense when we were first saved, we still need to repent of individual sins so that we don't return to them.

To repent means to 'turn away from' or to 'change your mind'. When we repent, we are pivoting away from sin, repulsed by its nature, whilst being empowered by the Holy Spirit to not walk back into it. It's here that we experience the truth of ***Romans 12:2 (NLT): "Don't copy the behavior and customs of this world, but let God transform you into a new person by changing the way you think. Then you will learn to know God's will for you, which is good and pleasing and perfect."*** The deceitfulness of the devil in tempting us to sin is exposed; our carnal behaviour is brought out into the light, and we no longer consider the sin as acceptable.

In general terms, the more we process the cleansing from sin out of a soft, humble heart, the more opportunities we'll have to spend in close proximity to God. But if you get stuck in worldly sorrow and think you've been forgiven, then you'll just be lukewarm and your heart will increasingly be hardened.

QUESTIONS TO PONDER

- **Describe in your own words the difference between godly sorrow and worldly sorrow.**
- **Have you ever exhibited worldly sorrow? When was that, and how did things turn out?**
- **What's the biggest sin you've ever repented of? How did you feel afterwards?**
- **Have you ever been—or are you currently—stuck in a sin-confess-sin cycle? What's stopping you right now from bringing this to the Lord so that you can repent of the sin and turn away from it, breaking its hold on you?**

WEEK 4 SUMMARY

Day 22: Distanced – The penalty for our sins has been paid so that we can be 'in Christ', but the consequence of sinning is a distancing from God—that's why forgiveness is essential.

Day 23: Exposing Sins – The devil wants to blind us to our sin because he knows it separates us from intimacy with God, reduces our effectiveness, and weakens our witness.

Day 24: Scammed – Satan uses the same old tricks to scam us into sin; once we fall for his lies and deceit, an ungodly chain reaction can so easily kick in.

Day 25: Grieving & Pleasing – As his children we can make our Father God both happy and sad, through faith and sin respectively.

Day 26: The Refining Process – Our pursuit of holiness is achieved by constantly identifying and eliminating sin in our lives.

Day 27: Idolatry – Idolatry can be alive and well today inside followers of Christ. Without realising it we can be worshipping the provisions of God above the person of God.

DAY 28: Getting Rid – Godly sorrow looks like worldly sorrow, but only the former leads to repentance.

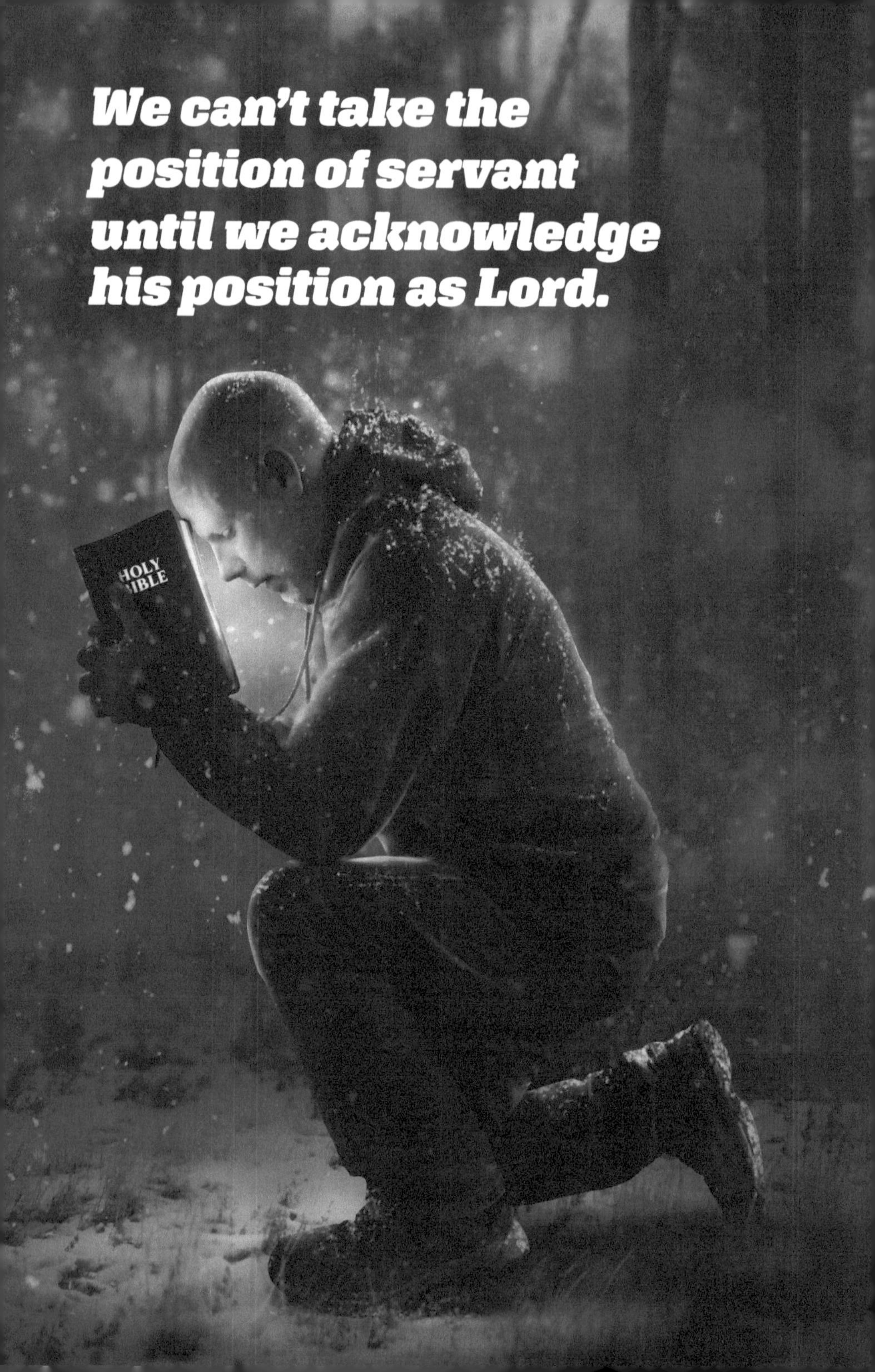
We can't take the position of servant until we acknowledge his position as Lord.
HOLY

WEEK

5

The doorway to intimacy: SERVANTHOOD

SERVING THE CREATOR

It was straight down to business for Adam in the garden. The first thing we see after God created him is recorded in ***Genesis 2:15 (NIVUK), "The Lord God took the man and put him in the Garden of Eden to work it and take care of it"*** (emphasis mine). God created man for his good pleasure and to share his love with him by means of a close, intimate relationship, but in the mix of that he had work to do. Adam didn't just sit in lush green pastures all day, gazing at waterfalls and singing melodies to God whilst in awe of his creation. He had a job. He got his hands dirty. His work was to upkeep the Garden of Eden (which incidentally wasn't a garden like we understand it, it was far greater). And he wasn't some kind of skivvy; he had additional responsibilities given him. In ***Genesis 2:19*** God brought all the animals on the earth to Adam and had him name them (what a day that must've been!).

Eden was a starting point. It would seem that a bigger expansion plan was on the table, for after he created humans God blessed them and said, in ***Genesis 1:28-30 (NIVUK), "'Be fruitful and increase in number; fill the earth and subdue it. Rule over the fish in the sea and the birds in the sky and over every living creature that moves on the ground.' Then God said, 'I give you every seed-bearing plant on the face of the whole earth and every tree that has fruit with seed in it. They will be yours for food. And to all the beasts of the earth and all the birds in the sky and all the creatures that move along the ground – everything that has the breath of life in it – I give every green plant for food.'"*** So God created mankind to rule over the earth. That was his plan right from the beginning, and it still is today.

The first instruction we just read was for Adam and Eve to multiply and fill the earth. That's certainly happened. We've gone from two people back then to eight billion today (in fact, that latest *billion* milestone was hit whilst writing this book—on 15th November 2022, if it ever comes up in a pub quiz).

So we've filled the earth with people bearing God's image, but we haven't been able to subdue it because of the fall and the outbreak of sin that went viral with it. Had Adam and Eve carried out God's commands, the world today would be full of people faithfully looking after God's earth. And maybe about now God would have seen the work as complete, with the whole earth entering the eternal state of Sabbath rest—that same rest we're waiting for today, when Christ returns for his millennial reign on earth.

BACK TO THE ORIGINAL PLAN

But even though we messed up as human beings, God's rescue mission was always in sight. His intention to dwell with a holy people in a holy land could not be thwarted by human sin. We particularly focused on that last week, seeing how sin works in our lives and how we can eliminate it. ***Ephesians 2:1-2 (NLT)*** says, ***"Once you were dead because of your disobedience and your many sins. You used to live in sin, just like the rest of the world, obeying the devil—the commander of the powers in the unseen world. He is the spirit at work in the hearts of those who refuse to obey God."*** You now serve a different master; you salute a different king. You once followed the ways of the world, living and adapting to its standards, but you now follow the legislation of heaven—the Bible—and follow *its* standards.

GROWING AS SERVANTS

God didn't need us to subdue the earth, but he instructed us to do it anyway. Why is that? Partly because he's calling us to obedience, and through that we develop our relationship with him. Through ongoing obedience we learn to trust him more—and he can trust us with more.

This also leads to personal growth. Every command God asks of us isn't just for his sake, but for ours. The call to obedience is for our benefit. He knows what's best for us and how to develop us to be stronger servants of Christ. Being a servant shouldn't be a burden but a joy; a way of worshipping God and growing in our faith.

If we want to experience the blessed life that God created us for, then we have to trust him as his servants. If we want the peace that surpasses all understanding, we have to give up the right to understand everything. That's not 'anti-understanding'; it's just a matter of getting our priorities in the right order. We surrender to his will first, then seek to understand after. Some people will only trust God when they understand him, but it's better to trust God solely because he's spoken, and *then* learn why as part of the journey of servanthood. The highest level of intimacy is trust.

The concept that you can control your destiny and evolve enough spiritually to make the right choices and run your own life is a lie from Satan. Yes, God has given us a free will to make choices in life, but they should be decisions that glorify God, not ones that gratify us. Yes, God wants to give us the desires of our heart, but we died to our own selfish gain when we met Jesus. He put *his* heart in us, so *our* desires are really the desires that he put in there. Someone once put it like this: 'The only thing that God has ever wanted of you was all of you!'

THE WEEK AHEAD

As we take our penultimate leg of this journey, we'll be putting our attention on how obeying God brings us closer to him.

You'll read the word *lordship* quite a bit. This simply refers to Jesus' reign in our lives. Just as a servant relates to a master, a student to a teacher or a member of staff to a boss, so should we relate to Jesus. He's our *leader* and our *Lord*.

This week we'll be examining how the same God can be both Saviour and Lord. We'll focus on our relationship with him as Lord and see how that affects our lives. We'll expose the essential element for a successful Christian walk: obedience. We'll touch on what place authority has in us being intimate with God. And we'll start to see the importance of keeping in step with the Spirit, before unpacking that further next week.

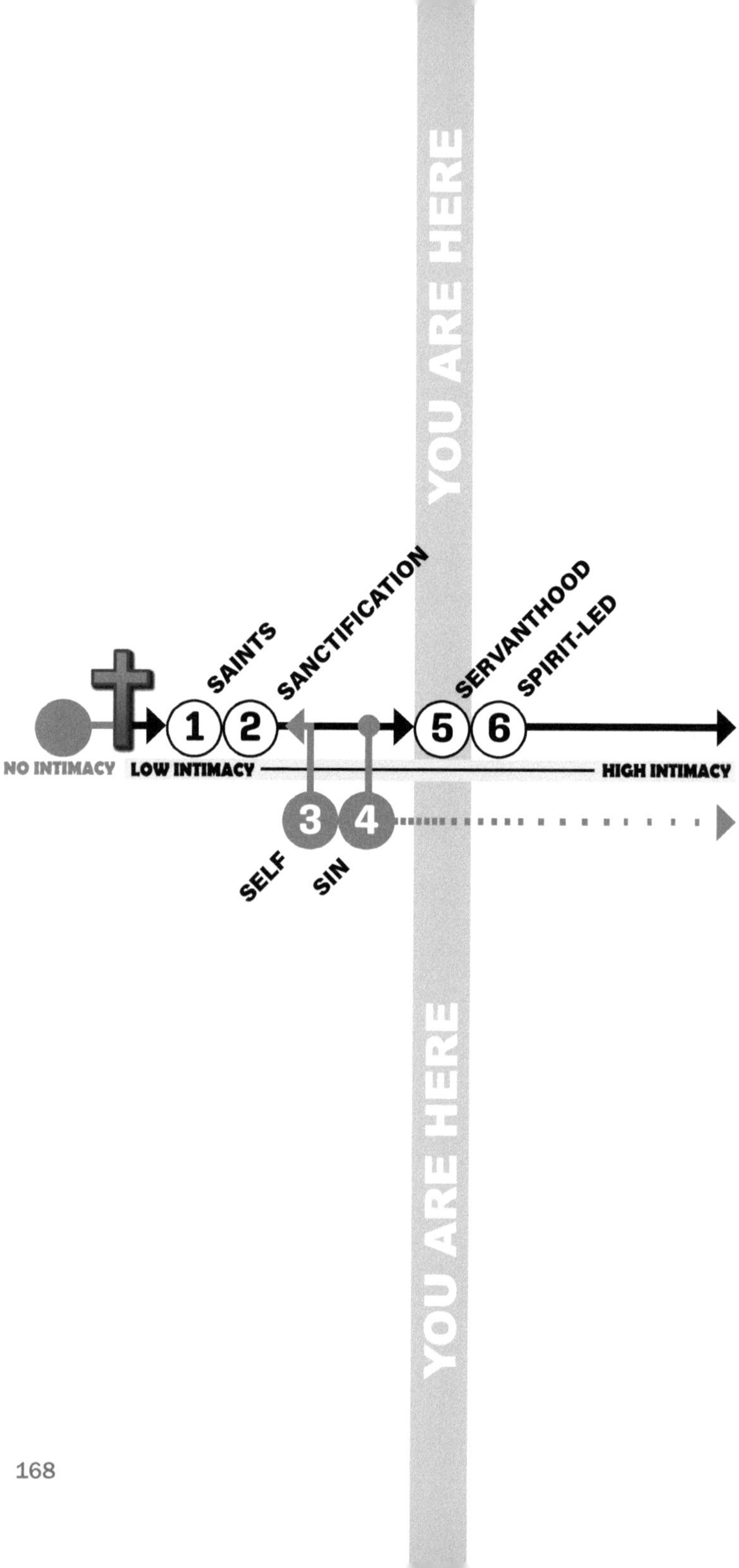
YOU ARE HERE
SAINTS
SANCTIFICATION
SERVANTHOOD
SPIRIT-LED
1
2
5
6
NO INTIMACY
LOW INTIMACY
HIGH INTIMACY
3
4
SELF
SIN
YOU ARE HERE

DAY 29

THE TWO TREES

LET'S DIVE STRAIGHT into the scriptures today, swimming all the way back to the conception of sin that we focused on last week. ***Genesis 2:8-9 (NIVUK)*** says, ***"Now the Lord God had planted a garden in the east, in Eden; and there he put the man he had formed. The Lord God made all kinds of trees grow out of the ground – trees that were pleasing to the eye and good for food. In the middle of the garden were the tree of life and the tree of the knowledge of good and evil."*** (By the way, to save on ink let's just abbreviate it to 'the tree of knowledge' from now on.)

Think about this for a moment: God never intended that we should know the difference between good and evil. Instead his plan was that we'd simply trust and obey him. This is the essence of lordship.

'But surely there's no harm in knowing the difference between good and evil? In fact, it might be good, right?' you may be thinking. Well, yes in one sense, but no in another.

It's good because we have a moral standard. We know it's wrong to kill, for example. But it's *not* good in that it can be subjective in certain situations—even ones that can cause divisions.

Take the 'murder' example and think about a potential dilemma for Christians who fought in World War Two. By the end of the conflict in 1945 the British Army peaked at around 3,000,000. In addition, around 61,000 had registered as a conscientious objector. Many of those were objecting to fight on religious grounds, not least standing on God's command: 'Do not murder'. However, out of the whole army there were an estimated 600,000 churchgoers who were prepared to fight—and ultimately kill—in defence of their country. So if you do the maths, for every six people who sat regularly under the teaching of the Bible, five were willing to put themselves in a position of taking someone else's life. There's obviously a huge amount of context needed to properly bottom out a statement like this—and I'm not saying what's right or wrong; I'm simply making the point that the dividing line between good and evil is not always clear cut, and can be open to interpretation.

THE TREE OF THE KNOWLEDGE OF GOOD AND EVIL

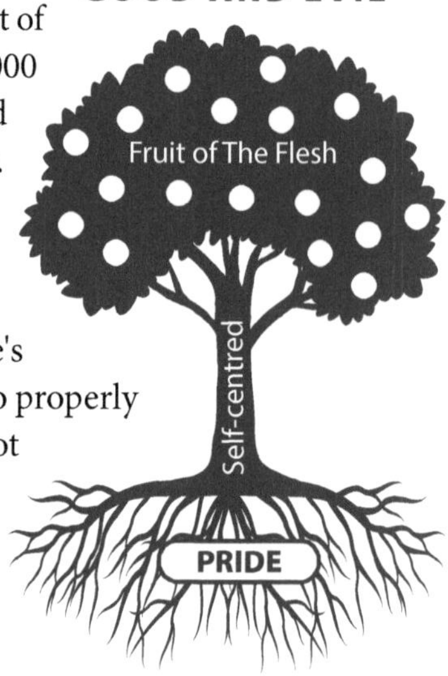

Think about churches. What one allows another might prohibit. This can cause difficulties and instability within denominations, movements and the Church at large. Even amongst Christians today there's an increasing number of issues that divide us—sexuality, abortion, equality and identity being some current hot topics.

If Adam and Eve hadn't eaten from the tree of knowledge our world would be so different. For starters, there'd be no sin. We'd be in the original, unspoilt, Edenic state, looking something like the Kingdom of God on earth. A Kingdom involves a King's domain. That domain is heaven invading earth. Jesus is King, and his word is final—no debating required, only total trust and obedience to his lordship. That's what we ultimately miss today in our walk with God. We so often think we know what is right and wrong because we have the knowledge of both. Add our personal subjectivity into the mix, and the lines can easily get blurred.

The good news is that we don't have to wait until the second coming of Christ for the cataclysmic mistake in the garden to be put right. King Jesus may not have returned yet in person, but he's fully here by the Holy Spirit. If you've put your faith in him, then he's living in your spirit right now. He can't get any closer.

This leads us once again to the area in our lives that we're constantly called to overcome: the flesh; the carnal nature; the old way of living; all the objections that rise up and oppose the directives of the Spirit.

You could argue in the same way that the two trees in the garden give us a foreshadow of the choices we have to make today. God instructed Adam in ***Genesis 2:17 (NIVUK), "You are free to eat from any tree in the garden; but you must not eat from the tree of the knowledge of good and evil, for when you eat from it you will certainly die."*** He could choose spiritual life or spiritual death. So too in the New Testament era we live in today, ***Romans 8:4 (NIVUK)*** says, ***"do not live according to the flesh but according to the Spirit."***

Although the flesh has nothing good in it, the tree of knowledge was not *bad*; it was just *forbidden*. But there is a common aspect in both: pride. Pride was in play when Adam and Eve chose to disobey God, and pride is the initiator every time we choose our flesh over God's Spirit. When pride takes root in our hearts, it will always manifest self-centredness at its core. We were created by God to love others as we love ourselves, but the devil is always out to totally oppose God's agenda.

The result of Adam and Eve eating of the tree of knowledge was death—spiritual death. Although Jesus has come so that we can have life again, we still have free will. We can still choose to taste death, even though we are alive in Christ.

The fruit of the flesh is listed in ***Galatians 5:19-21***; we'd do well to take daily stock of our motives and make sure we're not nurturing the ground around the wrong tree. If we do happen to bear such bad fruit, then thank God we can deal with it immediately. Through confession, such fruit is pulled off the tree and composted. But only through repentance does the root of pride get pulled up. If we don't add repentance to our confession, the sin is forgiven, but its DNA is still in the tree.

As we start a week focusing on the lordship of Christ in our lives, let's check that he's Lord not just in rhetoric but also in practice.

QUESTIONS TO PONDER

- **What part of your life might other Christians argue isn't godly? How sure are you that Christ is Lord in this area?**
- **Are there choices in your life on which you don't feel you need to consult God? If so, why not?**
- **What fruit of the flesh is lurking—hidden by the leaves of the tree of knowledge—that no one else can see but you? What's stopping you right now confessing that and asking the Spirit to help lead you into repentance?**
- **If Jesus stood before you in person and revealed the areas of even the smallest amount of pride in your life, what do you think he would identify?**

YESTERDAY'S SUMMARY: The lordship of Christ in our lives means nothing if it's just words; it needs to be a living, daily reality.

DAY 30

LORDSHIP

WE'VE TOUCHED ON 'making Jesus Lord' several times already—it's one of the central themes of this book—but now it's time to tighten our grip on the issue.

There's an old illustration about lordship which still works today. It goes something like this: when you put your faith in Jesus and make him Lord of your life, it's like you pick him up as a hitchhiker; but instead of simply driving with him on board, you move over to the passenger seat and let him take the wheel.

Think about that example in real life. You'd never allow anyone else to steer your life for you, would you? Even the most trusted friend or successful person you know wouldn't be invited to take *full* control. But Jesus is the perfect driver. He will never direct you the wrong way or cause an accident.

I think it would be fair to say that in this day and age of the

Church—especially within charismatic circles—we've made it easier than ever for people to accept Jesus into their lives. With a bit of soft music at the end of a sermon and an emotional invitation to repeat a 'sinner's prayer' to secure their ticket to heaven, why wouldn't someone want to accept the amazing free gift of eternal life? But what about counting the cost? What about future persecution? What about suffering? What about trials? What about the narrow way? Sure, there are huge benefits to following Christ, but there's also a cross that comes with every membership package. In ***Luke 14:27 (NIVUK)*** Jesus says that ***"whoever does not carry his cross and follow me cannot be my disciple".*** We're called to 'die to self' every day, and that means keeping Jesus as Lord.

Isaiah 53:6 (NLT) reminds us that, ***"All of us, like sheep, have strayed away. We have left God's paths to follow our own."*** Like the first car illustrated in the diagram, we were once heading our own way, unknowingly destined for destruction. Fuelled by our own selfish desires, we emitted a trail of loneliness, hopelessness, anxiety, hurt, anger and fear.

But God's rescue plan came in the form of his Son, Jesus. His name came up on our satnav. As we approached him he beckoned us to stop. There was nothing about his roadside appearance that attracted us to him (***Isaiah 53:2***), but deep down we sensed the need to pull over. As we engaged with him, something deep in our souls resonated—so much so that we put our faith in him.

We invited him into our car (life) as *Saviour* and to take the driver's seat as *Lord.* His first manoeuvre was a U-turn. Like the disciples on the road to Emmaus, our hearts burned within us as we started travelling with him, chatting along the way. He drove us to some thrilling, beautiful places. All of a sudden we were experiencing a totally new way of life. We were fuelled by the power of the Holy Spirit within us and what came out of us was love like we'd never experienced, peace that we couldn't fully explain, and a deep joy that remained despite our circumstances. We were happy for him to drive, to have him as Lord. We got settled in the passenger seat.

We fell in love with Jesus, we followed his commands as we learned

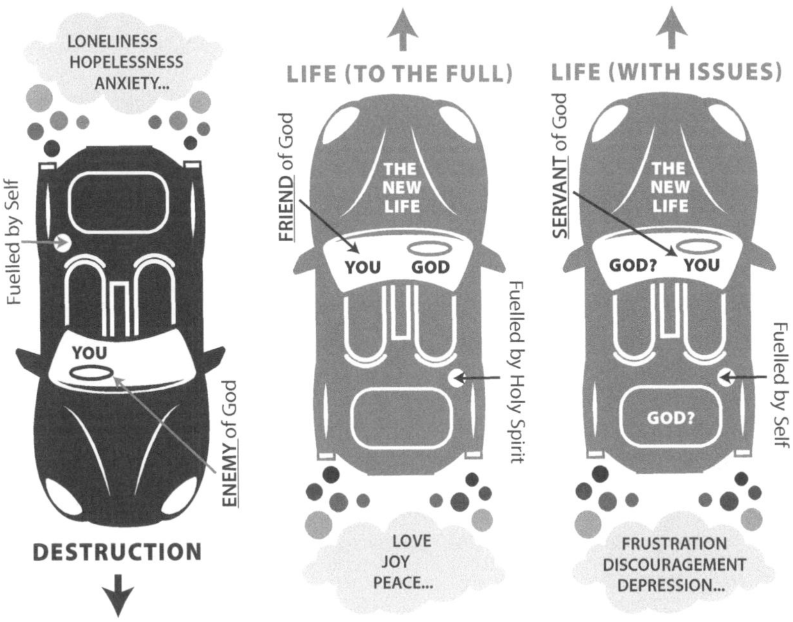

them and we sensed his presence. In ***John 14:23 (NIVUK)*** Jesus said, ***"Anyone who loves me will obey my teaching. My Father will love them, and we will come to them and make our home with them"***.

As we racked up days, weeks and months in the Kingdom, many of us unfortunately took some wrong turns without realising them. We were heading in the right *general* direction, but the longer we travelled, the more off-track we become. Some of us got cut up in the devil's traffic; we detoured off the road that God marked out for us. We've taken breaks at service stations, then decided to have a go at driving ourselves, moving Jesus over to the passenger seat. Maybe we've been hit and spun off the road and, blaming him, took back control of the car. Jesus has pulled some of us over onto the hard shoulder to deal with essential maintenance, but rather than confronting the issue we've just driven on ourselves.

Whatever the scenario, without Jesus in the driving seat of our lives we're only going to experience discouragement, depression, disillusionment, disappointment and a whole host of other 'd's that hold us back and stall our progress. Yes, we're still heading for heaven; we're still saved (for it was grace alone, through faith, that saved us), but we've gone back to relying on our own strength and our own wisdom.

For some it's even more severe, in that Jesus isn't even reduced to the passenger seat—he's been bundled into the boot! People want the security of heaven that a relationship with Christ brings, but they're happy living life their own way until that moment comes. What a travesty! What a mistake!

Others are content with Jesus just being on board, but don't understand what lordship is about. They have relative successes as a Christian and because of that boast that Jesus is good. They're sadly mistaken. As the Lord says in ***Jeremiah 9:23-24 (NLT), "Don't let the wise boast in their wisdom, or the powerful boast in their power, or the rich boast in their riches. But those who wish to boast should boast in this alone: that they truly know me and understand that I am the Lord who demonstrates unfailing love and who brings justice and righteousness to the earth, and that I delight in these things. I, the Lord, have spoken!"***

Just as we saw in Week One, day seven, God is both *holy* and *love*. Two sides to the same coin. So too he is both Lord and Saviour. Let's make sure he's fully in the driving seat of everything we think and do.

QUESTIONS TO PONDER

- **Where is the Lord Jesus in terms of today's illustration—is he in your driver's seat, the passenger seat, the back seat or the boot? Why?**
- **If he's not in the driver's seat, what will it take for you to get him back there? And what's stopping you doing that?**
- **How do you feel when Jesus has full control of your life and how do you feel when he doesn't?**

◀◀ **YESTERDAY'S SUMMARY:** For Jesus to truly be Lord, he has to be firmly in the driving seat of our lives.

DAY 31

LOSING LORDSHIP

YESTERDAY WE ENDED up looking at the difference between two cars that can represent our life in Christ. We're going to pick that up again and expand some more. So let's lift up the bonnets of these cars and see what's actually going on under the hood.

Referring to today's diagram overleaf, we can see that as Christians we all have Jesus as Saviour, but not all of us currently have him as Lord. There's a big difference, because without him as Lord our lives get littered with difficulties. The chances are that we did accept him as both Lord and Saviour at salvation, but as we noted earlier we can so easily end up taking back control of our lives. This could have been for a number of reasons. Here are three possibilities:

1. **We didn't fully realise what it meant for Jesus to be Lord.** No one really spelt it out for us. We never fully grasped that our lives

are no longer our own; that we were bought at a cost, belonging to him.

2. **We had a bad experience and fell out with God.** Maybe a loved one died unexpectedly, a relationship went south, or we had health issues. We still loved him deep down, but we stopped trusting him in this area of our lives. As the saying quite rightly goes, 'If he's not Lord of all, he's not Lord at all'.
3. **We were lured into sin by the devil.** We didn't submit to Christ's lordship and acted in the flesh rather than the Spirit. Without the Spirit's strength to enable resistance, we sinned. We felt bad. We got stuck in condemnation. We entertained worldly sorrow. We repeated the sin. Then again. And again. And… You get the picture.

Some people might not have lost the lordship of Christ in their life because it wasn't there in the first place! ***Luke 6:46 (NIVUK)*** records Jesus saying to his followers, ***"Why do you call me, 'Lord, Lord,' and do not do what I say?"*** (I love the way our Saviour is full of love and compassion, but at the same time says it exactly how it is!) People were saying one thing, but doing another. They had all the right labels on the outside, but on the inside they were a contradiction.

Whether we like to admit it or not, every time we walk in our own ways we walk in our own righteousness. We're saying our ways are good enough. To fully understand the actual worth of our own efforts towards right living we can go to ***Isaiah 64:6 (NLT),*** which says, ***"When we display our righteous deeds, they are nothing but filthy rags."*** The original Hebrew words used here are incredibly strong. In short, 'filthy rags' is a gentle

US CALLING THE SHOTS	**GOD** CALLING THE SHOTS
Revisiting Death	New Life
Heaven Like Brass	Open Heaven
Lack	Fullness
Nothing Good	All Spiritual Blessings
Our Righteousness	His Righteousness

translation. More literally, Isaiah is saying that our righteous acts are viewed by God as a 'soiled feminine hygiene product'! It's no wonder that the Apostle Paul said in ***Romans 7:18 (AMP)***, ***"nothing good lives in me, that is, in my flesh [my human nature, my worldliness—my sinful capacity]."***

In ***Ephesians 4:13 (NLT)*** Paul explains that we, the Church, will continue to be equipped until ***"we all come to such unity in our faith and knowledge of God's Son that we will be mature in the Lord, measuring up to the full and complete standard of Christ."*** This is our aim. Maturity. Fullness. Completion. All the things we explored in Week Two. This pursuit of holiness is steeped in blessing and favour. On this journey, the will of God comes hunting us down. It's where true fulfilment is found. But it can only be achieved by having Jesus as Lord.

Let's face it, the end result of us taking lordship of our lives is sin. ***Isaiah 59:2 (NLT)*** cuts to the chase: ***"It's your sins that have cut you off from God. Because of your sins, he has turned away and will not listen anymore."*** Now of course we're living under the New Covenant—so our sins are forgiven—but that doesn't negate the fact that God can't be associated with our sinful behaviour. He still loves us when we sin, but he doesn't like what we do.

When we walk in the flesh—following our old human nature—we lose the lordship of Christ in our lives. The more often we lose it, the more desensitised we become to the things of God. Then, before we know it, we don't even realise that God is not at the helm of our lives. And even if we did, we are deceived and don't deem it that important. This is damaging and will hugely minimise our effectiveness as Christians.

One final warning: Losing lordship can happen really fast. We saw last week how God miraculously delivered Israel from Egypt. ***Psalm 106:9-14 (NLT)*** summarises the account, ***"He commanded the Red Sea to dry up. He led Israel across the sea as if it were a desert. So he rescued them from their enemies and redeemed them from their foes. Then the water returned and covered their enemies; not one of them survived. Then his people believed his promises. Then they sang his praise."*** But a gear change of epic proportions takes place as the scriptures continue, ***"Yet how quickly they forgot what he had done! They wouldn't wait for his counsel!"***

They wouldn't wait for his next instruction. He'd guided them out all the way to this point, but as soon as they were free they didn't think they needed God's guidance any more. How foolish.

But let's take time out here for a reality check before we conclude today. Were we like that after we'd got over the initial excitement of our salvation? Can we be like that after a great victory in God? Maybe God gets us that promotion, delivers our healing or brings along our life partner. Do we suddenly act as if we don't need God that much any more?

To put it another way, have the blessings of God somehow made us self-sufficient? We may not see it, but it's definitely worth thinking about.

QUESTIONS TO PONDER

- **Has there been a time when you think you lost the lordship of Christ in your life? If so, what happened? How did it make you feel and how can you prevent it happening again?**
- **Do you think you might currently be deceived into thinking that Jesus is Lord of your life right now, when in reality you're calling the shots?**
- **Do you feel that you've sometimes had greater joy, peace and passion in God than right now? If so, what's changed? And how can you get that back?**

YESTERDAY'S SUMMARY: Losing lordship happens subtly without us realising it. We have to identify where it happened so we can put it right.

DAY 32

COUNTING THE COST

WE'RE GOING TO camp largely in one scripture today (Luke 14:25-33 NLT), and I'll be commenting as we go along. Let's get going...

Verse 25: "A large crowd was following Jesus". An early pause for thought to give some context. Jesus was a rabbi, which means *teacher*. When we think of teachers, we probably go in our minds to a classroom full of students sitting behind desks. This wasn't how a Jewish teacher operated back in first-century Palestine. Rabbis would move around in everyday life with their students (called *disciples*) following them. Teaching was often done 'on the job'. The disciples saw Jesus teach by example, first-hand, then they would go and do likewise.

The Lord was increasing in popularity; his followers were mesmerised by his miracles and amazed by his authority. But Jesus—on his way to Jerusalem, to face his executioners—wanted to make sure these followers knew exactly what standards were expected of them to continue in his ways once he was gone.

Verses 26-27: "He turned around and said to them, 'If you want to be my disciple, you must, by comparison, hate everyone else—your father and mother, wife and children, brothers and sisters—yes, even your own life. Otherwise, you cannot be my disciple.'" (Mic drop.) In one of his typical teaching moments that cut deep, Jesus gave them the bottom line of what it meant to be a disciple: prioritising him—in everything.

Let's be crystal clear. Jesus isn't telling us to hate our family or friends; he's simply drawing a contrast between loving *them* and *him*. The language being used is hyperbolic. He's saying that their love and commitment to him shouldn't just be more than to anyone else, but *so much* more. So much more that the comparison looks like the difference between love and hate. That's quite a gulf. But that's what Jesus requires. That's lordship.

And note that we ourselves are not exempt from this. Even the focus we give to our own lives should in contrast look poles apart from how fixated we are by Jesus' life. That's true lordship.

Verse 27: "And if you do not carry your own cross and follow me, you cannot be my disciple." This language and metaphor would be clear to the crowd listening. The only people who would be seen carrying a cross would be those on their way to crucifixion. When Jesus told his followers to carry their crosses he was giving them a death sentence—the constant killing of the flesh and resultant life in the Spirit.

Verse 28: "But don't begin until you count the cost." Jesus continues by giving a stern warning to anyone who may be thinking too much with their heart instead of their head. As if loving Jesus far above themselves—or anyone else—wasn't hard enough, and as if denying the flesh wasn't enough of a constant battle, there was another obstacle that Jesus put before his followers, just to make sure they were truly fit for service: counting the cost.

Let's not get confused here. The gift of eternal life is free to anyone

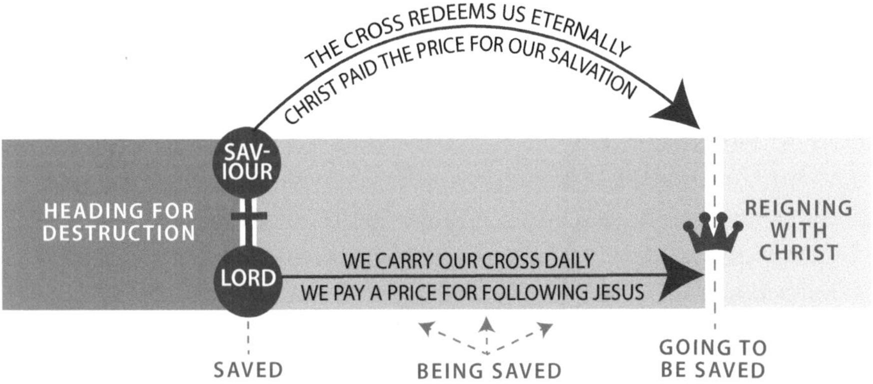

who believes (***John 3:16***); it's by faith that we're saved, through grace, not by any works done by us (***Ephesians 2:8-9***). We're saved when we put our faith in him. But that doesn't mean we're *following* him. We should be following him because he's worthy, because he first loved us, because he brought us to the Father, and because he never leaves us. But that's not always the case. We can get derailed by the devil, the world or the flesh.

Jesus then gives the first of two illustrations. ***Verses 28-30: "For who would begin construction of a building without first calculating the cost to see if there is enough money to finish it? Otherwise, you might complete only the foundation before running out of money, and then everyone would laugh at you. They would say, 'There's the person who started that building and couldn't afford to finish it!'"***

Jesus is saying, "Get past the current excitement of being saved; get past the prospect of final salvation in eternity. Now focus on the journey in between—the 'being saved'. It's going to cost you. Not just for the short-term foundational work, but for the whole build." God wants to develop something incredible with your life. Are you willing to pay the price?

Here's the second illustration. ***Verses 31-32: "Or what king would go to war against another king without first sitting down with his counselors to discuss whether his army of 10,000 could defeat the 20,000 soldiers marching against him? And if he can't, he will send a delegation to discuss terms of peace while the enemy is still far away."***

Here Jesus is telling us again that it's not always going to be a walk in the park. There are going to be times when it seems like the odds are stacked against us. But when we partner with God, we receive the ultimate counsellor—the Holy Spirit. He empowers us for battle. He gives us the strategies for victory.

Sometimes I can't help but think that some invitations to receive Christ are just 'easy'. Part of me wants that because I don't desire anyone to go to hell—not even my worst enemy! But I think, like Jesus, we need to fully present the *hard* part too: giving up everything.

And so Jesus' discourse ends with ***verse 33: "So you cannot become my disciple without giving up everything you own."*** That's a hard statement to swallow from a natural viewpoint, but from a spiritual one it's like, 'Why wouldn't you—when you stand to gain so much more?'

QUESTIONS TO PONDER

- **When you accepted Jesus as your Lord and Saviour, how much did you understand about his lordship? What was missing?**
- **When was the last time that following Christ cost you something? How did it go? How did you feel?**
- **What does 'carrying your cross daily' mean to you?**
- **Can you, hand on heart, say that you love Jesus infinitely more than yourself, your spouse, your partner or any family member? If not, why not?**
- **What would it take for you to be radically on fire for God? What's stopping you?**

YESTERDAY'S SUMMARY: A spiritual decision to follow Jesus shouldn't just be based on emotions; it needs to be carefully weighed up.

DAY 33 — OBEDIENCE

THERE'S AN OLD hymn written by John Sammie in 1887. The opening verse goes like this: *"When we walk with the Lord in the light of His Word; What a glory He sheds on our way! While we do His good will, He abides with us still; And with all who will trust and obey."*And, if you know the tune, sing along to the chorus now: *"Trust and obey, for there's no other way; To be happy in Jesus, but to trust and obey."*

Biblical obedience is more than simply doing the right thing. The original words translated 'obedience' in the scriptures carry with them the essence of hearing, trusting, submitting, and surrendering to God and his Word.

Obedience is so important for us today. It always has been. We've already seen how a disobedient Adam and Eve set off a wave of consequences. As a result, God had to give the Ten Commandments to try and keep his people on the straight and narrow. ***Deuteronomy 11:27-28 (NKJV)*** sums up the situation: ***"Behold, I set before you today a blessing and a curse: the blessing, if you obey the commandments of the LORD your God which I command you today; and the curse, if you do not obey the commandments of the LORD your God, but turn aside from the way which I command you today, to go after other gods which you have not known."***

Thank God that the curse was removed through the sacrifice of Jesus (***Galatians 3:13***)—but does that mean we're guaranteed blessings? Only if we fulfil the criterion of obedience. This universal truth is echoed in the New Testament: ***Luke 11:28 (NLT)*** declares, ***"blessed are all who hear the word of God and put it into practice."*** It's true that we're blessed with every spiritual blessing when we accept Christ, but those blessings are only manifested when we align ourselves with Jesus and follow through with his instructions. ***James 1:25 (NLT)*** confirms this: ***"if you look carefully into the perfect law that sets you free, and if you do what it says and don't forget what you heard, then God will bless you for doing it."***

Obedience really is key. It's more important than the *seemingly* spiritual side of our life in Christ, such as fasting, offerings and sacrifices. But simple obedience is what God wants above everything. Even a well-intentioned sacrifice is not worth more than following through with what we know to be right. ***Jeremiah 7:21-23 (NLT)*** reports it like this, ***'This is what the LORD of Heaven's Armies, the God of Israel, says: "Take your burnt offerings and your other sacrifices and eat them yourselves! When I led your ancestors out of Egypt, it was not burnt offerings and sacrifices I wanted from them. This is what I told them: 'Obey me, and I will be your God, and you will be my people. Do everything as I say, and all will be well!'"'*** It couldn't be much simpler than that, could it?

The simple instructions around obedience continue into the New Testament. For example, Jesus is quoted in ***John 14:21 (NLT)*** as saying ***"Those who accept my commandments and obey them are the ones who love me."*** Anyone can say they love God, but are they obeying him according to the truth revealed in the scriptures? Are they forgiving everyone they need to, free of grudges and bearing with people who annoy them?

Are they regularly in church gatherings? Are they praying for other believers and encouraging others instead of speaking negatively? Are they submitting to those in authority and faithfully giving to their local church? We could go on, but you get the picture. Here's the reality: the more you love and trust God, the more you will obey him.

You're the servant of whoever you obey. Who do you go to for ultimate guidance in life? Maybe it's a spouse, parent or preacher. Maybe it's a friend, mentor or pastor. But normally it's either God or it's yourself (no prizes for guessing the best person to choose).

The disciples were servants. They went through all kinds of trials and hardships as they sought to obey Jesus. They didn't always get it right, but in the end they all came good (with the exception of Judas!). They learnt obedience. They trusted Christ. As a result, Jesus called them friends, and started to disclose the secrets of the Kingdom. ***John 15:15 (ESV)*** shows us this, ***"No longer do I call you servants, for the servant does not know what his master is doing; but I have called you friends, for all that I have heard from my Father I have made known to you."***

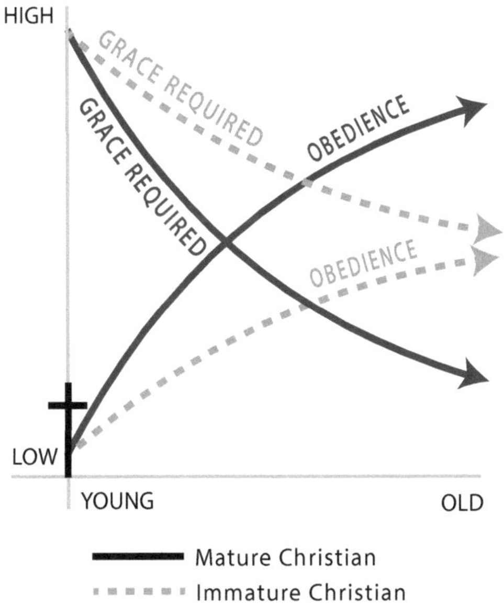

Jesus said this right at the end of his earthly ministry on the day before he was crucified. The disciples had been with him three-and-a-half years before the 'no longer' came. No longer were they living by their own rules as *servants*, but now they were following the commands of Christ as *friends*. They were still serving God in the general sense, but they entered into a new dimension of their relationship. Abraham (***James 2:23***) was known as a friend of

God; so too was Moses (***Exodus 33:11***). You and I can also be known in heaven as friends of the Lord by obeying God.

In ***James 4:4 (NLT)*** the Apostle James gives some straight talk (just like his half-brother, Jesus, often did): ***"You adulterers! Don't you realize that friendship with the world makes you an enemy of God? I say it again: If you want to be a friend of the world, you make yourself an enemy of God."*** The sad reality is that we can be born again but not be friends with God. And if we're not friends with God, we're friends with the world.

1 John 2:3 (ESV) says, ***"And by this we know that we have come to know him, if we keep his commandments."*** Rewind almost five weeks. On Day One we learned that eternal life is all about knowing God. That *knowing* is intimate. Today we end by seeing that the same *knowing* can only be achieved through obedience.

QUESTIONS TO PONDER

- **When was the last time God told you to do something that you followed through with? How did that go?**
- **What has God previously told you to do that you currently haven't done? What's stopping you doing it, and how can you overcome that?**
- **Do you feel you're more a servant of God or a friend of God? How would you describe the difference?**
- **How different do you think your life would be if you readily obeyed God every time? Does that vision of a better life in God stir you to serve him more faithfully?**

YESTERDAY'S SUMMARY: Obedience is better than sacrifice, and it proves that we truly love God.

DAY 34

AUTHORITY

I LOVE THE prayer of the Apostle Paul to the church at Ephesus. Let's read it in ***Ephesians 1:18-21 (NIVUK): "I pray that the eyes of your heart may be enlightened in order that you may know ... his incomparably great power for us who believe. That power is the same as the mighty strength he exerted when he raised Christ from the dead and seated him at his right hand in the heavenly realms, far above all rule and power and dominion, and every name that is invoked, not only in the present age but also in the one to come."*** We see here that God raised Christ from the dead and sat him at his right hand (which is the place of *all rule and power*) and this is why Jesus is King! That's good news. But there's more.

In ***Ephesians 2:6 (NIVUK)*** Paul also says that, ***"God raised us up with Christ and seated us with him in the heavenly realms in Christ Jesus."*** Did you catch that? I hope so. Because if you get this incredible truth etched into your heart, your Christian walk may never be the same again.

Consider this: there's no place in the New Testament where we're told to ask God to do anything about the devil. Why is this? Because we're seated with Christ in the place of all power and it's *our* job to exercise authority. God has delegated this responsibility to us.

We can hear this commissioning of power through the words of Jesus a couple of times in the gospels. Firstly, ***Luke 10:19 (AMP)*** instructs us, ***"Listen carefully: I have given you authority [that you now possess] to tread on serpents and scorpions, and [the ability to exercise] over all the power of the enemy (Satan); and nothing will [in any way] harm you."*** That's pretty clear.

Secondly, in his great commission Jesus tells his disciples in ***Matthew 28:18 (AMP)***, ***"All authority (all power of absolute rule) in heaven and on earth has been given to Me."*** That echoes the sentiment of Paul's prayer to the Ephesians which we opened with. Matthew continues by saying that we're to take that authority and collectively change the world! ***"Go therefore and make disciples of all the nations [help the people to learn of Me, believe in Me, and obey My words], baptizing them in the name of the Father and of the Son and of the Holy Spirit."***

Furthermore, we read in Mark's account of the great commission (***Mark 16:17-18 NIVUK***) that ***"these signs will accompany those who believe: In my name they will drive out demons; they will speak in new tongues; they will pick up snakes with their hands; and when they drink deadly poison, it will not hurt them at all; they will place their hands on sick people, and they will get well."*** When we understand that we're seated with Christ in the place of all authority and that we have power over demons, the power of God to speak in a heavenly language and the power to transfer the healing power of Christ onto others, then that's when we really start to live out our salvation the way God intended us to.

We could automatically be led to think that this kind of living would be only available to gifted apostles, pastors, teachers, prophets or evangelists who have been following Jesus for years; but no, we're told that these are the signs that indicate someone is a believer—anyone. Very soon after being born again, a new Christian can walk in these ways if they grasp the truth of the Bible, rather than believing the lies of the devil.

As we mature in God, our level of authority can grow also. It works like this: to the same extent that we allow God to have authority over us, we have authority over the devil. Consider ***Luke 7:2-10 (NLT)*** as an example, ***"At that time the highly valued slave of a Roman officer was sick and near death. When the officer heard about Jesus, he sent some respected Jewish elders to ask him to come and heal his slave. So they earnestly begged Jesus to help the man... But just before they arrived at the house, the officer sent some friends to say, 'Lord, don't trouble yourself by coming to my home, for I am not worthy of such an honor. I am not even worthy to come and meet you. Just say the word from where you are, and my servant will be healed. I know this because I am under the authority of my superior officers, and I have authority over my soldiers. I only need to say, 'Go,' and they go, or 'Come,' and they come. And if I say to my slaves, 'Do this,' they do it.' When Jesus heard this, he was amazed. Turning to the crowd that was following him, he said, 'I tell you, I haven't seen faith like this in all Israel!' And when the officer's friends returned to his house, they found the slave completely healed."***

Can you imagine Jesus being amazed? Well, he was. And it was all over a display of faith. The faith that widened Jesus' eyes was all down to the fact that it was exercised from a man who understood authority.

Here's the principle again, put more succinctly in ***James 4:7 (AMP), "So submit to [the authority of] God. Resist the devil [stand firm against him] and he will flee from you."*** If you truly have Jesus as Lord over all your life, and if you're submitting to the delegated authorities over you (such as pastors, bosses, the police and governing officials), then you can command the mountains in your life to move and the storms to still.

Do you have sickness? Submit to God and rebuke the devil. Are you weighed down with oppression? Command your problems to go. Don't let any fear, doubt or condemnation usurp your authority.

Victory may not come straight away; if it doesn't, persist. And whilst you stand firm, unwavering in faith, listen to the Holy Spirit who will guide you to victory. He may be wanting to bring you understanding about your situation that you're unaware of and need to pray into. Don't waver in the knowledge that God has placed you with Christ in the place of *all* power.

It sounds too good to be true, I know—but the devil knows it's not, and if he can keep you from that truth then he can limit your effectiveness and dampen your experience of *being saved.*

QUESTIONS TO PONDER

- **If the level of authority you have is directly connected to the level of authority you submit to, how are you faring under God's delegated authorities in your life?**
- **How do you feel when your pastor or minister says something you don't like or you don't agree with? Do you still submit to them?**
- **What 'mountains' are in your life right now? What's stopping you from commanding them to move?**

YESTERDAY'S SUMMARY: To have authority you've got to come under God's authority, which includes his delegated authorities in your life.

DAY 35

THE TWO YOKES

IF I SAID that you'd been 'yoked', would you understand what that means? You might be forgiven if you thought you'd been attacked by a group of kids using eggs as their weapons of warfare.

Yoke is a word that's still used today, but nowhere near as much as it was 2000 years ago when it was written in the scriptures. Back then, 'to be yoked' was an everyday farming term. A yoke was a long piece of wood (see overleaf) designed to join two animals, such as oxen, to walk together in unison. A load—often a plough—could be hitched to the centre of the yoke, resulting in the combined strength of the two animals being able to do more than both individual efforts.

In some of the most recognised words of Jesus, he says in ***Matthew 11:28-30 (NIVUK), "Come to me, all you who are weary and burdened, and I will give you rest. Take my yoke upon you and learn from me, for***

I am gentle and humble in heart, and you will find rest for your souls. For my yoke is easy and my burden is light." These verses may be well known, but are they fully understood? In headline terms, Jesus calls us to *walk* with him, and to *work* with him. But let's dissect this somewhat more to fully understand why Jesus chose this agricultural metaphor.

When two animals were yoked together, one would be experienced (the *master*), and one would be somewhat inexperienced (the *servant* or, more accurately, the *slave*). The latter would learn how to position themselves in the yoke, what posture to adopt, and how to move in time when it came to speed and stride. Jesus is the master. We are the servants. As we journey with him through life, we learn to walk in step with him—not going ahead, not slacking behind. In basic terms, whatever we see Jesus do, we too should do.

If our lives aren't positioned for worship, if our posture isn't shaped with humility, if we're not fitted ready for forgiveness, then we'll feel discomfort as the yoke chafes on us. This is what happens to any animal that isn't copying their lead partner in how they carry themselves.

If being yoked to Jesus allows us to understand how to navigate this world effectively, why wouldn't we want to be taught by having him constantly by our side? Well, as we've seen several times already, our old carnal nature needs bringing under control. It wants nothing to do with this nurturing, productive life with God. In fact, before we came to Christ, we were *yoked* to the world, unknowingly a slave to its ways. ***Galatians 5:1 (AMP)*** mentions the comparison, ***"It was for this freedom that Christ set us free [completely liberating us]; therefore keep standing firm and do not be subject again to a yoke of slavery [which you once removed]."***

Hebrews 12:1 (ESV) also refers to the weight of

sin and our old way of living: ***"Therefore, since we are surrounded by so great a cloud of witnesses, let us also lay aside every weight, and sin which clings so closely, and let us run with endurance the race that is set before us."***

Thank God that we've been freed from the world, and we've been brought to our Lord Jesus to whom we gladly swore allegiance; but the world, the flesh and the devil continually throw all they can at us to try and disconnect us from Christ. If we're not relying solely on Jesus, then we can find ourselves coming out from under his yoke. We may still be ploughing the field of salvation, but we're largely unproductive. We tire, we lack joy and we're often void of peace.

This is why trust is vital; it's why faith in the process is of paramount importance. Where trust is high, growth is fast; when trust is low, growth is slow. When Jesus said his yoke is easy, he's saying it fits perfectly. The Greek word translated 'easy' also means *good* and *useful*. Jesus' yoke has no negative connotations; it's hugely beneficial. Our mission in life is simple: be discipled and make disciples of others. Without being yoked to Christ, we're not going to get very far at all.

Finally, 'his burden is light'. The Jewish audience listening to Jesus were taught to keep over 600 laws that their religious leaders concocted. It was an arduous task. But Jesus doesn't demand *works* to enter the Kingdom of God; he just requires *faith*. When we're yoked with Christ, the burden is light because he took up the heavy load of sin on the cross after living a perfect life. And he continues to take the strain for us, in that when we sin we're just a prayer away from forgiveness.

On the rare occasions that I'm out walking with Kate (she doesn't like walking!) she'll link arms with me. It's nice. It feels good.

It shows partnership and connection. It doesn't actually *achieve* anything most of the time, but if we get to a steep hill, I'll tense my frame, tighten the link of our connected arms, and drive forward with more energy. In doing so, I'm taking the lead, but we're still both perfectly in step. Because Kate's fully connected to me, she doesn't have to exert herself as much because she's drawing from my energy. That's kind of how it is when we're tight with Jesus, walking in step with him. He takes the bulk of the load.

Wearing the yoke of Jesus certainly isn't a fashion accessory, but it *is* an essential part of Christian living. If we're not connected to the power source we're living life in our own strength—and that's hard work! And when we achieve anything *we're* getting the glory, not God.

As we close out this week's focus, let's make sure Jesus is our chief ox, our senior partner, our Lord and our Master.

QUESTIONS TO PONDER

- **What's stopping you getting up close and personal with Jesus right now so he can take the weight of any load you're currently carrying?**
- **We can't be yoked with Christ *and* carry on sinning, so what sin might be in your life that is unconfessed?**
- **What differences are there between you and the way Jesus walked, talked, and generally conducted himself? What one thing will you commit to, in order to become more like him?**
- **What was the last thing that you relied on Jesus for, and what's going to be the next?**

WEEK 5 SUMMARY

Day 29: The Two Trees – The lordship of Christ in our lives means nothing if it's just words; it needs to be a living, daily reality.

Day 30: Lordship – For Jesus to truly be Lord, he has to be firmly in the driving seat of our lives.

Day 31: Losing Lordship – Losing lordship happens subtly without us realising it. We have to identify where it happened so we can put it right.

Day 32: Counting the Cost – A spiritual decision to follow Jesus shouldn't just be based on emotions; it needs to be carefully weighed up.

Day 33: Obedience – Obedience is better than sacrifice, and it proves that we truly love God.

Day 34: Authority – To have authority you've got to come under God's authority, which includes his delegated authorities in your life.

Day 35: The Two Yokes – Walking in step with Jesus makes life easier and lighter; walking in our flesh is harder and heavier.

If your life isn't
supernatural,
it's superficial.

WEEK
6

Our walk of intimacy:
SPIRIT-LED

INTIMACY

You should have it fully installed in you by now that this book has *intimacy with God* at its core. It's mentioned on the front cover and it runs right through to this last section.

In our last week together, we'll be looking at how to be led by the Spirit. Being sons and daughters of the living God is an unfathomable privilege; becoming like him is an honour. If that were the end goal, then in comparison to our former lives we would be satisfied. But it's not. There's more. There's always more with God.

Yesterday we laid a foundation for the week ahead by looking at how we're yoked to Christ. We saw how being intrinsically connected to the Lord means that we can obey him when he speaks. But in our last few days we'll investigate how he speaks, and how we can hear God with our *spiritual* ears.

Communication is the essence of any natural, thriving relationship, and it's no different in our relationship with the Lord.

A LOVE FEST

The eternal plan of heaven was to share the fellowship experienced amongst the Godhead (Father, Son and Spirit) with a global community of human beings.

The love of God that perpetuates from the Trinity has now been injected onto the earth through the person of Jesus Christ. For this love virus to become pandemic, the Son of Man in his body of physical limitations (he couldn't be in several places at once) had to ascend back to heaven to eventually tag the Spirit of God. In turn, he pours out himself to everyone who calls on the name of the Lord, wherever they are (he's omnipresent). ***Romans 5:5 (NKJV)*** tells us that, ***"the love of God has been poured out in our hearts by the Holy Spirit who was given to us."***

This love encases many things, not least purpose. God has a will for every person who has been born—and will be born. First of all, that they do not perish but come to know him (the starting point of this journey we've taken together). From there, he has an assignment: a general one of living by faith, living in hope, and walking in love; and a specific one designed for each of us to accomplish according to the gifts and personality he's given us.

WORK TO DO

In my experience, the Church at large has traditionally focused much on the more general 'walk of God', but has somewhat neglected the more specific 'work of God' that we are all called to do. If we're going to fulfil the individual purpose of our life and know the Lord's will for us, then we need to hear his voice.

As human beings we're designed to manage, we're formed to produce, we're created to multiply. What we do, how we do it and when we do it are all essentials in terms of us being effective, productive and fruitful.

ETERNAL REWARDS

Our commanded works for God bring him pleasure because we're obeying his instructions—doing our small part in the bigger picture of his master plan; that's certainly a motivating factor, as we've already seen. But our efforts also bring us eternal rewards.

It's my experience that Christians don't think about eternity as much as they should. The Bible is clear about two particular things: 1) that this life has a direct bearing on our life in eternity, and 2) that our life in eternity is going to look similar to this one—we'll still have a body (which will be glorified), and we'll still live on earth (albeit a new earth, with a new heaven on it).

Our life on this planet is like a click of a finger compared to eternity. ***James 4:14 (NIVUK)*** echoes this truth with one of the Bible's quickest 'question and answer' times, ***"What is your life? You are a mist that appears for a little while and then vanishes."*** If this life is so short then surely we should make the absolute most of it? In order to maximise every moment on earth, we need continually to be close to the Lord, ready to obey whatever instruction he gives us and enjoy the thrill of partnering with the King of the universe.

EVERY LITTLE STEP

Just like God led Israel in the desert using a pillar of fire by night and pillar of smoke in the day, God leads us too. He doesn't need to communicate externally through pyrotechnics and smoke signals any more though; he's directing us internally by his Spirit. ***Romans 8:16 (NKJV)*** tells us that ***"The Spirit Himself bears witness with our spirit".***

In ***John 5:19 (NIVUK)*** Jesus said, ***"the Son can do nothing by himself; he can do only what he sees his Father doing"***. So too we should be learning to discern what God's good, pleasing and perfect will is for us, and follow it.

It's worth noting that Christ didn't just do specific tasks that he saw God doing; it wasn't just the odd conversation or assignment here or there that God told him to do; Jesus *couldn't* (not *didn't*) do anything of his own accord. This doesn't mean that we always hear everything perfectly. ***1 Corinthians 13:9 (NLT)*** says, ***"Now our knowledge is partial and incomplete, and even the gift of prophecy reveals only part of the whole picture!"*** But we *can* know his ways, and we *can* hear his voice.

It's important also to understand that we aren't being led by God merely as *slaves*, but as *sons* and *daughters*. ***Romans 8:14-16 (NLT)*** reminds us, ***"For all who are led by the Spirit of God are children of God. So you have not received a spirit that makes you fearful slaves. Instead, you received God's Spirit when he adopted you as his own children. Now we call him, 'Abba, Father'."*** We won't always get it right, but he would much rather we tried to walk in the Spirit, getting it wrong, than not have the faith or courage to take a step at all.

COMING UP…

Within our final few days together, we'll be looking at the ways God speaks to us, as well as the ways we can more effectively hear him. We'll see how we can test the words we receive to make sure it's God speaking. And we'll end up looking at how God is not just our personal God, but a corporate one, of the Church.

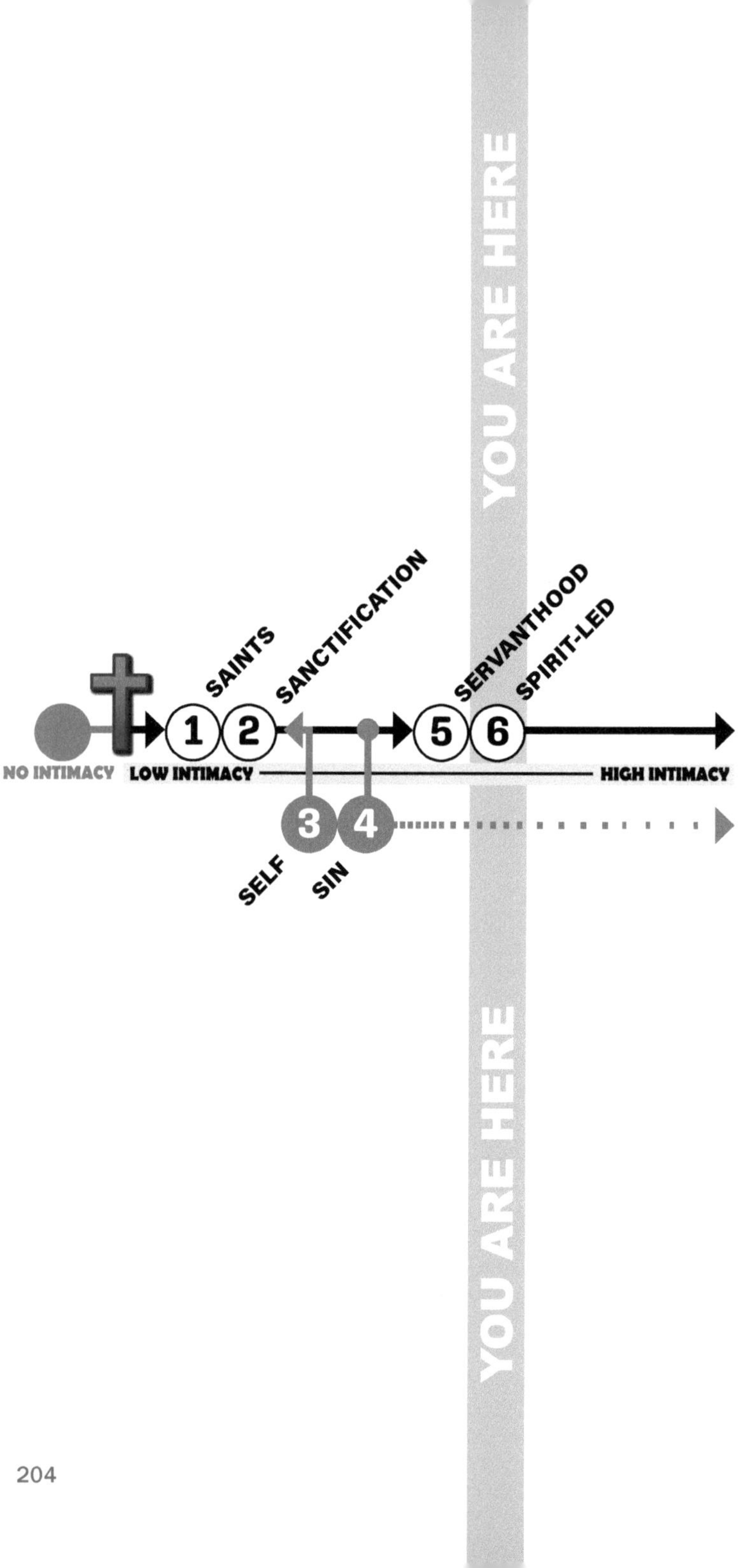
YOU ARE HERE
SAINTS
SANCTIFICATION
SERVANTHOOD
SPIRIT-LED
1
2
5
6
NO INTIMACY
LOW INTIMACY
HIGH INTIMACY
3
4
SELF
SIN
YOU ARE HERE

DAY 36

PACE-SETTING

MY RECENT VISITS to the Accident & Emergency Centre have led me to learn more about the cardiovascular system, in particular why my heartbeats suddenly felt more like a morse-code message than a regular sinus rhythm. I found out that it's all to do with electricity.

Did you know that your body's blood pump is reliant on electrical power to keep it going? I'm not sure I did. Like most of us, I took it for granted that when it beats it does it again a second later, and again, and again… In fact, since my pulse came into being in the womb over half a century ago, my heart has just kept beating—around a billion and a half times to date. I've never had to remind it, never had to persuade it, never had to coerce it.

It's all thanks to something called the SA node: the tiny electrical power pack of cells at the top of your heart. It's more commonly known as the 'pacemaker'. Its job is fairly simple: send a charge through a network of special branch-like cells that contract the upper chamber of the heart; within the same circuitry, one of the branches connects to the AV node. Similarly, another network of branches makes the bottom half of the heart contract. So the top half of the heart contracts, squeezing the blood into the bottom half; this then contracts, pushing the blood out of the heart, and around the body it goes.

There's a small but crucial part of this whole process that prevents it from all going wrong—an ever-so-slight (tenth of a second) delay of the electrical current passing through the AV node. Without this, the whole heart would be flooded with blood; with it, there's a perfect regulation of blood flow.

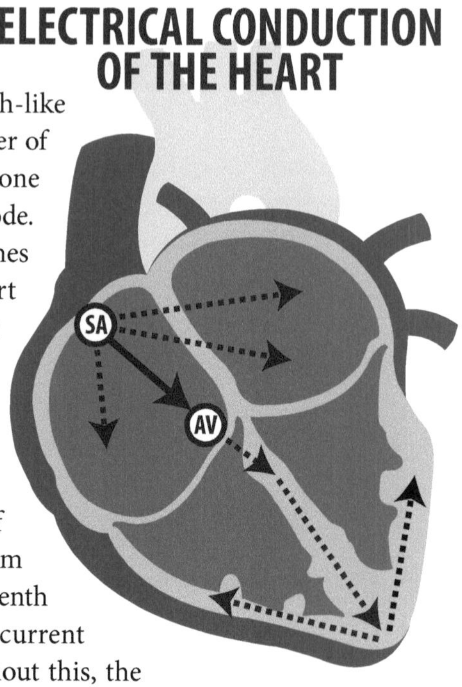

This subtle, but vital, delay is largely unnoticed because it's all really part of the same heartbeat. This is very much like what we saw yesterday with being yoked to Christ, in that when he moves we should follow. But there's another facet here that we can learn from being in step with the Spirit: pace. When he speeds up we should speed up; when he slows down we should slow down.

Just as there are times when we rush around and our heartbeat increases to allow the required extra oxygen to pass through our system, so too there are times when we need the extra breath of the Holy Spirit to be in us so that we can accomplish everything we need to in God.

The Holy Spirit is our perfect pacemaker. But in our busyness we can often unyoke ourselves and keep running ahead when God has slowed down. If we keep that up for too long, then we're in trouble—not just physically, but spiritually also. The one thing I've learned the hard way is that you don't often hear God when you're busy. His voice is rather heard in the daily moments that you take to settle your soul and focus on him. And in the increasing pace of life that we all seem to be facing in one way or another, those extended times of annual leave are also crucial—not just for physical rest and relaxation, but for spiritual enlightenment and revelation.

It's no wonder that God puts such importance on the Sabbath—that weekly 24-hour break from the bump and grind of the week; that place where we get rested, refocused and re-energised for the week ahead. It's only in recent times that I've started to draw on this necessity on a meaningful level. As a pastor, I've succumbed to the deception that being busy for God might not be a *good* thing, but it can't be a *bad* thing. It is! It's easy to think that God doesn't mind because it's all for him. But he does. It's a sin.

I've never been an anxious person, but I've been a stress expert. Now, it's good for your body to have a degree of 'good' stress; it gets the adrenaline pumping and can aid achievement. But maintain that for too long and it turns bad, evil and sometimes even deadly. No one on their tombstone has the inscription, 'I wish I'd spent more time in the office'.

When we outpace the Spirit, we're going too fast—whether slightly or a lot. We become so driven by time pressures that we leave zero room for creativity or spontaneity. Even when we do things 'for God' we can end up missing ministry opportunities whilst we serve him.

Margin is essential for a Spirit-led life. If we're constantly running from one assignment to the next appointment, we're not going to hear God much. Don't kid yourself otherwise.

One thing we can do to win back some time is to work sharper. ***Ecclesiastes 10:10 (AMP)*** puts it like this, ***"If the axe is dull and he does not sharpen its edge, then he must exert more strength; but wisdom [to sharpen the axe] helps him succeed [with less effort]."*** When life is pressuring you and it feels like there's not enough time to do everything, you need to stop and work out how you can achieve all that God has asked you to do in the time you have. Sometimes we need to work sharper, but at other times we need to just *stop* the work.

Saying no is not easy for many, especially Christians who genuinely want to serve God. But if we did only what the Spirit told us to do, we'd continue to walk with him, at his pace. If he thinks we should take on something more and trust him to empower us, then we definitely should. Equally, if he says to stop something, then we should do that also. It's not always easy, but it's simple.

We've all been given the same wonderful gift of 24 hours in every day, but some of us abuse it. Let's maximise this gift of time by moving only when we see the Holy Spirit moving, whether that's at a normal pace, faster pace or slower pace. As **Matthew 11:29-30 (MSG)** says, ***"Walk with me and work with me—watch how I do it. Learn the unforced rhythms of grace. I won't lay anything heavy or ill-fitting on you. Keep company with me and you'll learn to live freely and lightly."***

QUESTIONS TO PONDER

- **When was the last time you asked God if you were going ahead of him?**
- **Do you have margin in your life? If not, how can you create it?**
- **What work might God be asking you step up into, or release yourself from?**
- **Are you getting a healthy balance of work, rest and recreation in your life? If not, what one thing can you commit to do to change that?**

YESTERDAY'S SUMMARY: Keeping with the pace of the Holy Spirit is essential for our wellbeing and spiritual productivity.

DAY 37

HOW GOD SPEAKS

SO MANY PEOPLE have a relationship with God, but the key to intimacy is communication. If a husband and wife hardly talk then the marriage may be functioning in name only. It's the same with believers.

My guess would be that people are generally familiar with speaking to God (prayer), but struggle to hear him. So today we're going to briefly look at five ways that God speaks to us. Using my experience, and that of others, I'm presenting them in order of what I believe is most common.

1. THE BIBLE

John 1:1 (NLT) says, ***"In the beginning the Word already existed. The Word was with God, and the Word was God."*** A few verses later we see in ***verse 14*** that, ***"the Word became human and made his home among us."*** So Jesus is the Word of God. All of the Old Testament points to the life, death and resurrection of Christ that we find in the gospels; all of the New Testament points back to his life, death and resurrection, and to his future return. Just as Christ spoke when he came in human form, so too the whole Bible is the essence of God speaking through his Son. ***2 Timothy 3:16 (AMP)*** tells us that, ***"All Scripture is God-breathed [given by divine inspiration]".***

If we open the Bible and in faith let it speak to us, it will. Every time. Whether you listen to it in audio format, scroll through it on your device or read the scriptures in a good old-fashioned book format, what you take in is God's primary way of communicating with you. Knowing this it's devastating to think that so many Christians don't prioritise it. I don't know about you, but I need it every day of my life. I'm not good enough to go it alone. I realised this some years ago; as a result I produced a journalling system that helps people to hear God through the scriptures. There's a sample in the appendix.

2. INNER PEACE

Colossians 3:15 (AMP) says, ***"Let the peace of Christ [the inner calm of one who walks daily with Him] be the controlling factor in your hearts [deciding and settling questions that arise]."*** The Greek word translated 'controlling factor' literally means *umpire*. Like a referee making the call in a football game, so God's peace can show you whether something is 'fair play' or 'foul play'.

Situations often arise in life on which we need God's guidance, so we offer them up to God in prayer. Sometimes scripture can't give us a specific answer, but the peace of God can. Maybe it's a decision that needs to be made about a job offer, a house purchase or a relationship involvement. God will either leave you feeling unsettled or peaceful. Therein may lie your answer.

3. OTHER PEOPLE

We've seen how God speaks to us directly into our spirit, but sometimes he will use other people to get there.

Spiritual authorities in our lives are important to listen to. Pastors, preachers, teachers, leaders, mentors—whoever you position yourself under. The person won't be perfect and you won't always agree with them, but that doesn't mean that God won't use them to speak into your life. He will.

Other Christians can also speak the will of God into your life. Even something as simple as a passing encouragement can be from the heart of God. Someone may give you a Bible verse that God put on their heart. Others may speak a prophetic word to you.

Whatever 'word' you receive, it's important that you weigh it up and test it as the Bible itself tells us to do. ***1 Thessalonians 5:19-22 (MSG)*** says, ***"Don't suppress the Spirit, and don't stifle those who have a word from the Master. On the other hand, don't be gullible. Check out everything, and keep only what's good. Throw out anything tainted with evil."***

4. CIRCUMSTANCES

Because of my recent health episodes, I did some fresh studying on what the Bible says about physical healing. I also looked at the reasons why people don't receive healing, although I've always believed that God wants us all physically well. As I re-engaged with the scriptures God spoke to me from ***Romans 12:12 (NIVUK): "Be... patient in affliction".***

Through this and other scriptures, God was teaching me how healing isn't always seen immediately and sometimes we have to be patient before it's fully manifested. Now God didn't make me ill to teach me that, but he used the situation to speak to me.

God speaks to us through particular circumstances. You may find yourself compelled to contribute financially when you hear of someone's need. God may tell you to prophesy over someone you're speaking to. In the forgiveness you receive, he might remind you of the unforgiveness you hold towards someone else. The possibilities of God speaking through our situations are plentiful.

5. DREAMS & VISIONS

We mentioned back on Day 13 about setting ourselves up for God not just to protect our thoughts as we sleep but also to speak to us in the night. 'Day' dreams (or visions) can also come to us—maybe when we're intensely focusing on the Lord, when we're worshipping or when we're reading the Bible. Several times in the Old Testament we see God giving people dreams and visions—think Abraham's star-filled sky, Jacob's ladder and Joseph's sheaves of corn. We see instances in the New Testament, too, as well as the more general prediction of scripture in ***Acts 2:17 (NIVUK), "In the last days, God says, I will pour out my Spirit on all people. Your sons and daughters will prophesy, your young men will see visions, your old men will dream dreams."***

In late 2019 one of the members of my church prophesied that God was going to talk to me through dreams. I was ready and expectant, but nothing happened immediately. However, after a couple of months, two incredibly vivid dreams came within 10 days of each other. One was specific about our church vision, and the other was about the Covid-19 virus that was brewing in the background. Both have shaped significantly the way we have led the church.

As well as my 'top five', it's worth mentioning that the Bible records God speaking through creation, angels, an audible voice, and even once through a donkey! It doesn't matter so much *which* way God speaks; what matters is that we understand that we *can* hear his voice. ***John 10:27 (NKJV)*** says, ***"My sheep hear My voice, and I know them, and they follow Me."***

QUESTIONS TO PONDER

- **How often do you hear God speak?**
- **In what ways has God spoken to you?**
- **Are you putting enough time into reading God's Word to hear from him? If not, why not, and how might you put that right?**

YESTERDAY'S SUMMARY: God speaks to us primarily through the Bible, so we must read this regularly to keep our relationship fresh, dynamic and productive.

DAY 38

TUNING IN

WE'RE GOING TO follow on from yesterday by looking at how we receive God's word. In the church age we now live in, God is always speaking to us.

He is an all-mighty and all-powerful God, and sometimes in the Bible his voice matches that. God spoke to Moses within the thunder of Mount Sinai, and Job's prayer was answered in a whirlwind. But as well as being a God to be revered, he's also relational. So God's voice, like in any loving relationship, can come in a conversational way, even a still small voice, like it did to Elijah at Mount Horeb. God can speak with differing intensities. And as we saw yesterday, the format in which God speaks can be different.

With that as the backdrop, let's now start to understand *how* we hear God's voice. Not how he speaks, but how we hear. We're going to use an illustration of a *radio* to do this.

Let's start with the radio station: God FM, if you like. ***Psalm 121:4 (NLT)*** tells us that he ***"never slumbers or sleeps"***. As God is always speaking, then this station is broadcasting 24/7. So wherever we are, and whenever it is, God is always speaking to us.

From our point of view as believers we're always plugged into the power source, because Paul said in ***Romans 8:11 (NLT)*** that, ***"The Spirit of God, who raised Jesus from the dead, lives in you."*** And ***Matthew 28:20 (NIVUK)*** says, ***"I am with you always, to the very end of the age."*** But even though we're connected, we still need to switch on. This is done by faith. We turn on the possibility of hearing God by trusting that he will speak. If we don't believe he'll speak, then we won't hear him.

So we're in Christ, and we're in faith. But there's still one essential thing to do: tune in. We do this by praying, listening, reading our Bible and so on. The tuning process classically happens during a devotional time or quiet time that we set aside to be alone with the Lord. It might also happen in a church service or prayer meeting. In fact, it can happen any time that God is being given pre-eminence. Sometimes it can take some fine tuning to clearly hear what he is saying; this can be achieved by either prolonged prayer or fasting.

Some people get frustrated at this stage because they just can't seem to get clarity from God. Commonly it's because they hold offence and unforgiveness in their hearts. This is like the equivalent of not having the radio's aerial up and extended. No matter how much you fine tune, the broadcast won't be heard. God takes this seriously. ***Colossians 3:13 (NLT)*** tells us, ***"Make allowance for each other's faults, and forgive anyone who offends you. Remember, the Lord forgave you, so you must forgive others."***

It may actually be that you're hearing God to some degree, but it seems a bit muffled, going in and out of signal. If so, you may be on the wrong frequency. If you have pride in your life, for example, it's like you're only receiving in a weaker *AM* frequency. But when you live in humility, you receive in a superior quality *FM* frequency. Some people have had pride in their heart all their Christian life and as such they just assume that God never speaks clearly. He does. Always. Until you switch to humility,

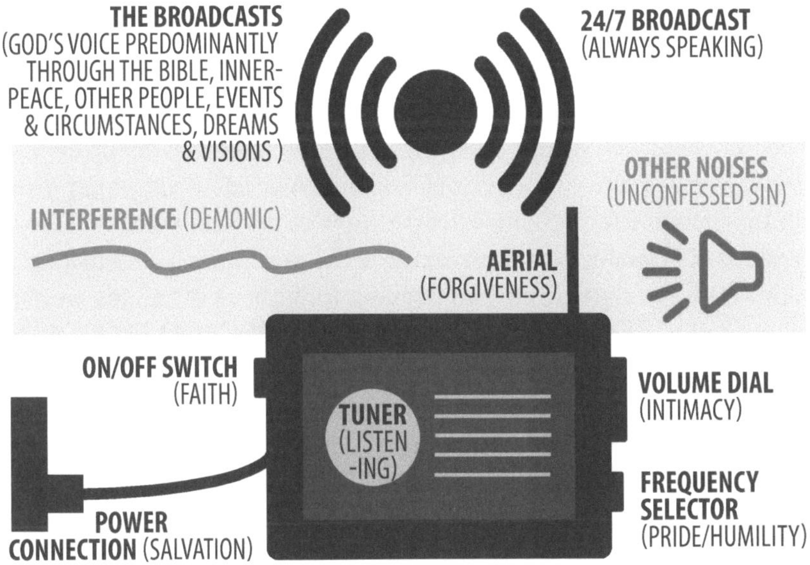

you'll never hear God properly. ***Hebrews 3:15 (NLT)*** states, ***"Today when you hear his voice, don't harden your hearts as Israel did when they rebelled."*** Israel was proud; they thought they didn't need God. Let's not make the same mistake by living in our own strength and wisdom. (And if you're thinking, 'Where's the perfect *digital* frequency?' well, we'll be tuned into that in our heavenly state when sin is finally eliminated.)

Something else that may hinder you from properly hearing God's voice may be external noises. This is what it's like when we have unconfessed sin in our lives. ***1 John 1:9 (NKJV)*** reminds us, ***"If we confess our sins, He is faithful and just to forgive us our sins and to cleanse us from all unrighteousness."***... and I'll add here, 'giving us ears to hear what the Spirit is saying'.

And on occasion other interference can be experienced via demonic influences. Until this is removed (by prayer, and sometimes with fasting), there will never be a clear transmission coming through. ***Mark 9:29 (NKJV)*** gives us Jesus' response to the problem when his disciples couldn't deliver an evil spirit manifesting in a boy. ***"He said to them, 'This kind***

can come out by nothing but prayer and fasting.'" We don't need to go looking for the devil round every corner but equally, as ***2 Corinthians 2:11 (NIVUK)*** tells us, ***"we are not unaware of his schemes".***

Finally, when you get tuned in, you'll soon want to pump up the volume. To make sure you're hearing God both *loud* and *clear*, simply dwell in his presence more. Take extended time to connect with him. Don't rush away. Worship him. Pray through the night. You'll do whatever it takes once you start tasting his goodness. In the book of Exodus, we read about Joshua, the young assistant of Moses. ***Exodus 33:11 (NLT)*** tells us that, ***"Inside the Tent of Meeting, the LORD would speak to Moses face to face, as one speaks to a friend. Afterward Moses would return to the camp, but the young man who assisted him, Joshua son of Nun, would remain behind in the Tent of Meeting."*** Joshua would continue to linger in the presence of God. He developed such a passion that he was hungry to get even the *crumbs* of his presence.

So the good news today is that you *can* hear from God, and you have the strategies to turn on and tune in to his voice, blocking any interference that may be around.

QUESTIONS TO PONDER

- **Do you struggle to hear God clearly? If so, could it be that you have pride or unconfessed sin in your life?**
- **What would your life be like if you heard from God clearly, on a regular basis? What benefits would that bring you?**
- **Have you identified any potential barriers to hearing his voice today? If so, what are they, and how might you be able to deal with them right now?**

YESTERDAY'S SUMMARY: God is always broadcasting, but we're not always receiving.

DAY 39

THE MIND OF CHRIST

OVER THE LAST couple of days we've looked at how God speaks (broadcasts), and how we can better hear him (tune in). Today we're going to realise that we don't have to wait for God to speak—we can know his thoughts constantly!

In ***1 Corinthians 2:16 (NLT)*** the Apostle Paul quotes from the Old Testament, ***"Who can know the Lord's thoughts? Who knows enough to teach him?"*** These words from the prophet Isaiah were originally written to speak of the majesty of God. The prospect of someone being in a position to instruct or teach the Lord is a ludicrous one, but that's a deliberate style of the writer to stress God's sovereignty.

Many have quoted this verse to make the point that God is far greater than we are and that his thoughts are way above ours. Although that thought was being presented in the Old Testament, Paul is using it to say something totally different in the New. It's not that he's taking away from the truth that it originally had, but he's adding to it.

If you only reference the quote from Isaiah you miss the radical point of what Paul is conveying. There's actually a bit more to the verse that we've not read yet... ***"But we understand these things, for we have the mind of Christ"*** (emphasis mine). I don't know whether you caught the full force of that; if you did, it's actually a pretty mind-blowing statement.

Paul is basically telling us that the things that Jesus thought when he walked the earth we can think too!

In ***Isaiah 30:20-21 (NLT)*** the prophet says to the rebellious nation of Israel, ***"Though the LORD gave you adversity for food and suffering for drink, he will still be with you to teach you. You will see your teacher with your own eyes. Your own ears will hear him. Right behind you a voice will say, 'This is the way you should go,' whether to the right or to the left."*** It doesn't matter how badly behaved you may have been, God is always wanting to teach, instruct and guide you. We don't have to wait for a *'thus sayeth the Lord'* prophecy; we can know what he wants of us immediately. Why? Because the Spirit of Christ is living inside us, and that includes his mind.

In ***Jeremiah 10:23 (AMP),*** we see another prophet speaking in a similar vein, ***"O LORD, I know that the path of [life of] a man is not in himself; It is not within [the limited ability of] man [even one at his best] to choose and direct his steps [in life]."*** He's saying that even the most intelligent, wise man at the top of his game doesn't have the ability to choose the right direction for his life. Again, that is true; he can't, not by himself. But we can, because we have access to the mind of Christ!

Yes, God speaks in all the ways that we looked at the other day, but when we're in an intimate state of relationship we can know his thoughts as the Spirit of God communes with our spirit ***(Romans 8:16).***

It's important to realise that the immaterial mind is separate to the material brain. Without Christ, your thoughts are your own. They are a product of the world around you. When you focus on something, your brain will process it and your body will act accordingly. And when you

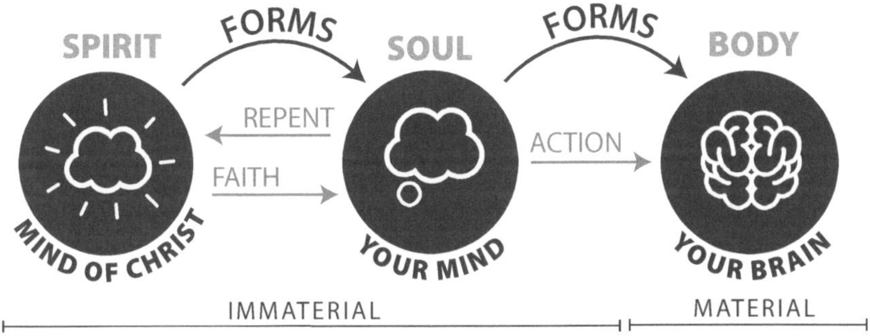

repeatedly think about something it actually creates small branch-like cells in in your brain called *dendrites*. After several weeks these become a permanent new feature of your brain that electrical circuits can easily pass through. Without Jesus they can easily become bad habits, but when we choose to be influenced by Christ's thoughts then good, godly neural pathways are formed so that we can naturally act out what God desires.

Interestingly, to repent literally means 'to change your mind'. We change our thinking to come in line with Christ's thinking. And the mind of Christ is a reflection of the Bible, so when we operate it by reading the scriptures we receive faith that we can act upon. As ***Romans 10:17 (NKJV)*** says, ***"faith comes by... the word of God."***

In late 1994 a girl who had studied at the same college as me walked into the small church where I was the associate pastor. During our former years in education we were more acquaintances than friends. Nevertheless, there was a connection we could build upon. We caught up, and chatted each Sunday. She'd had a radical experience in coming back to God, very much like the prodigal son parable. Her life had been steeped in sex, swearing, spirits (the drinking kind) and soccer. Regarding the latter, she was a full-on Nottingham Forest fan in every way you can imagine—she lived and breathed Brian Clough's Red and White Army.

With this in mind, you can understand why when I saw a Christians in Sport event advertised in our town, featuring ex-Forest striker (now turned evangelist) Phil Starbuck as guest speaker, that it made total sense to get two tickets. It wasn't a date. Not like that anyway.

We had a great time, so much so that we decided to go out again the next night, this time with a few of the young adults in our church. We all headed out for food. A bit of a pattern seemed to be emerging as we all found ourselves at the cinema the following night. Then my newfound footballing fanatic friend actually came to watch me play in a scheduled game I had the following night. It was only at this point that it seemed like something might be going on between us. This was confirmed on the fifth consecutive night when we were together, this time alone. I can't remember any of the conversation at all but I do remember God directing my path, just like the prophet Jeremiah described.

I didn't hear God speak as such, but I just knew with the mind of Christ that she was going to be my wife. So I asked her if she'd marry me, there and then. She knew too. She said 'yes'. I need to stress that I would never counsel anyone to do what I did, but in that moment of *knowing* I experienced very simple, but very powerful, peace and affirmation in my spirit. It was a potentially *dangerous* way of living, but equally *dynamic*. That's how it should be.

I'd love to say that my life is constantly full of me exercising the mind of Christ. It's not. But it *can* be. And God *wants* it to be. We have the fulness of Jesus living inside us, and that includes his mind. So by faith, let's allow his thoughts to form our thoughts.

QUESTIONS TO PONDER

- **What's the difference between *your* mind and the mind of Christ?**
- **How can you tap into the mind of Christ?**
- **Can you recall situations in which you have discerned the will of God? If so, how did you know it was God, not you?**

YESTERDAY'S SUMMARY: When we exercise the mind of Christ we think God's thoughts and can therefore do his will.

DAY 40

FASTING

WHEN IT COMES to hearing from God, fasting will aid us in that pursuit, especially when we're praying about specific and important things.

This ancient spiritual practice is as effective today as it's ever been. Unfortunately, though, it's not as popular as it's always been. Maybe people don't value God's presence as much as they used to? Maybe the discipline is just not taught as much these days? Or maybe people are just hungrier than they've ever been!

Whatever the situation, fasting will bring you closer to God. Here's the principle behind the practice: you remove the focus from the physical things of this world to concentrate on the spiritual. Put another way: fasting directs our hunger towards God. ***Matthew 4:4 (NIVUK)*** says, ***"Man shall not live on bread alone, but on every word that comes from the mouth of God".*** We put the natural under submission to move our

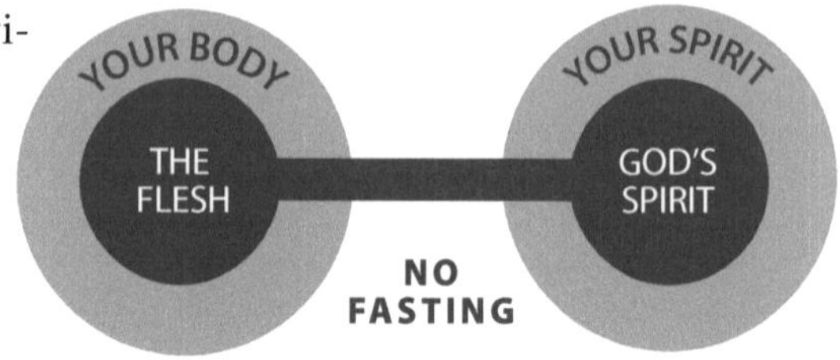

dependence onto the spiritual. Or if you want it more succinctly: we starve our flesh to feed our spirit.

Fasting isn't a spiritual hunger strike where we petition God to submit to our demands; fasting is about us humbly submitting to his commands. Fasting doesn't change God; it changes us.

So what do we do whilst exercising 'nil by mouth?' Well, fasting only really bears fruit if it's accompanied by prayer. Having said that, we can see other spiritual practices going on in the Bible when people fasted. In ***Nehemiah 9:1-3 (NLT)*** there was the reading of God's word, confession of sins and worship: ***"the people assembled again, and this time they fasted... they confessed their own sins and the sins of their ancestors. They remained standing in place for three hours while the Book of the Law of the Lord their God was read aloud to them."*** In ***Luke 2:37 (NLT)***, we see Anna the prophet serving God whilst regularly fasting: ***"she lived as a widow to the age of eighty-four. She never left the Temple but stayed there day and night, worshiping God with fasting and prayer."*** In ***Acts 13:2 (NLT)*** church leaders were worshipping and fasting when God broke in. ***"One day as these men were worshiping the Lord and fasting, the Holy Spirit said, 'Appoint Barnabas and Saul for the special work to which I have called them.'"*** So there are no hard and fast (no pun intended) rules as to what we should do whilst fasting, but prayer is a main activity.

As well as spiritual practices, there are practical things that can help you. Drink water—plenty of it. Plan where you'll be—avoid the kitchen as much as possible. Remove temptation—you're still human. Fast with someone else—it's a great way to stay accountable and encourage each other.

During a fast you'll increasingly experience a heightened sensitivity to God. I remember once during a fast I entered our church building where secular music was being played. The music wasn't demonic in any way;

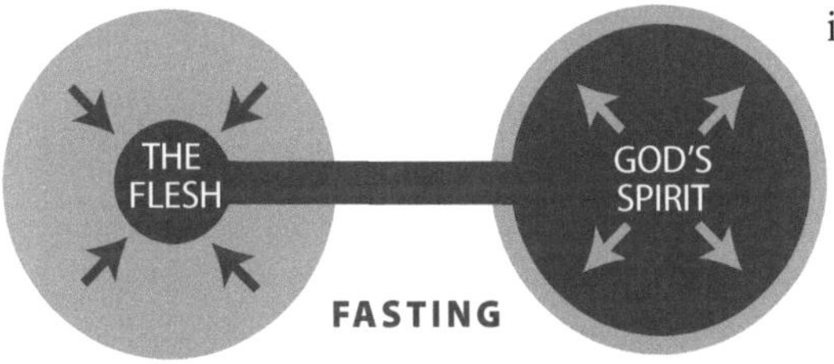

it just wasn't glorifying God. Any other time, I might not have said anything and just thought that someone was enjoying a bit of music, but the fasting had amplified my awareness of both the natural and the supernatural. During a fast you'll be able to better discern the will of God and generally be more tuned into the things of heaven.

It's worth mentioning that although fasting is seen in the scriptures as the giving up of food, you could consider eliminating other things in order to focus on God (e.g. social media, Netflix, TV, secular music). However, a biblical fast has its origins in food. Think of it like this: the first meal after a prolonged time overnight without food is called breakfast, because that's when you *break* your *fast.*

But even within traditional fasts there are different types. Firstly, there's the **partial fast**. This is a restriction of diet, rather than total abstinence. We see this in ***Daniel 10:3 (NKJV), "I ate no pleasant food, no meat or wine came into my mouth, nor did I anoint myself at all, till three whole weeks were fulfilled."*** Secondly, there's the **regular fast**. This is no food at all but taking water. And finally there's the **extreme fast**, which is no food or water. This fast is not to be entered into lightly—especially one with any substantial length of time—and should only be undertaken if you have a clear call from God. Even then, I strongly suggest it's approved by your pastor or minister. (And it's worth mentioning here that if you have any medical condition you should consult your doctor before fasting.) If you can't fast, it doesn't mean you will miss out. ***1 Samuel 16:7 (NIVUK)*** tells us that, ***"man looks on the outward appearance, but the Lord looks on the heart."*** Besides, this would be a good opportunity to do a different type of fast, such as we've already mentioned.

If you've never fasted before, I would recommend that you start by fasting for one day, or maybe even try skipping a single meal first. Get your mind, body and spirit used to this new activity. You can then build from there as you feel led.

If you truly desire to fast, schedule it in. This will help you commit to it and help you clear your diary accordingly. And before you start, segue yourself in by eating lightly the day before. It's also good to know what's coming, especially if you're going past a few days. If you are, day one will come fairly easily with practice, on day two headaches may come and go, on day three your brain starts to understand that you're not feeding your stomach as usual and, interestingly, day four onwards can feel like you're in a spiritually healthy rhythm with hunger not being an issue.

Other than the spiritual realm, fasting has physical benefits too. For instance, fasting for three days can regenerate your entire immune system. And after five to seven days your tastebuds refresh, giving you a new-found love for simple foods like fruit and vegetables!

There's also a psychological benefit. Fasting can break habits. Your gut is often referred to as your *second brain*. Starving the stomach for just a few days can break eating habits, drinking problems, drug abuse and other 'lusts of the flesh'. There's even research showing that fasting increases retention of information—this is good news if you regularly forget where you put your keys!

So *should* you fast? I could say yes from a scriptural point of view, but I think a better question to ask you would be: *'How much of God do you want?'*

QUESTIONS TO PONDER

- **Have you ever fasted before? If yes, how did you feel, and do you think you should do it more often? If no, could you commit to starting?**
- **Who could you speak to about joining you for a fast, and what would the purpose be?**

YESTERDAY'S SUMMARY: Fasting minimises our dependence on the natural so as to intensify the spiritual.

DAY 41

TESTING THE VOICE OF GOD

WE'VE CONCENTRATED THESE last few days on how God communicates with us. Let's draw that to a close today as we seek to understand how best we can confirm whether we've actually heard God's voice—rather than our own thoughts, or the language of the enemy.

If you're receiving a prophecy from someone, if you're getting a sense in your spirit, or—as we touched on on Day 39—if you believe you're activating the mind of Christ, not everything will hit a spiritual home run.

As we grow in God we learn to hear his voice more and more, but we'll never get it right all the time so it's always good to test the feelings and thoughts we believe are coming from God. To help us with that, we're going to answer three questions today. Here they are:

1. Does it agree with the scriptures?

God's *will* is never going to contradict his *Word.* (That's tweetable.) For example, if you think that the Government acts unrighteously, you may believe that God doesn't mind if you don't pay your taxes. But that's not God, because in ***Matthew 22:21 (NLT)*** Jesus spoke to the Pharisees' disciples about this issue and told them, ***"give to Caesar what belongs to Caesar, and give to God what belongs to God."*** And Paul bluntly says in ***Romans 13:6 (NLT), "pay your taxes"***.

Hebrews 4:12 (NLT) says, ***"the word of God is alive and powerful. It is sharper than the sharpest two-edged sword, cutting between soul and spirit, between joint and marrow. It exposes our innermost thoughts and desires."*** It's in the soul that your thoughts take place, and it's in the spirit where the mind of God is. These two invisible realms co-exist inside you and it can sometimes be hard to determine whether *you* are the source of your thinking, or *God*. But the Bible has the ability to separate the two clearly.

We also have to tread carefully here, because we can shoehorn scriptures into our situations to make them fit. Such words may be invalid, because they've been either taken out of context or misinterpreted. Rather than looking for a verse to validify a thought, it's much better to have a verse come to mind. ***John 14:26 (NLT)*** tells us that ***"when the Father sends the Advocate as my representative—that is, the Holy Spirit—he will teach you everything and will <u>remind</u> you of everything I have told you"*** (emphasis mine). Searching for a scripture isn't bad, but having the Spirit of God bring a verse to memory is best. This is why faithfully reading and learning the scriptures day by day is so important as it gives the Spirit a wealth of knowledge to work with. But this does take time to build up, so if you're a relatively new believer you may want to enlist the help of a mature Christian to help you discern. ***Ephesians 3:10 (NIVUK)*** says, ***"His intent was that now, through the church, the manifold wisdom of God should be made known".*** There are people in your church who live with enough integrity, and speak with enough honesty, to counsel you. They could be a mentor, a small group leader, elder or pastor.

2. Do I sense God's peace?

God's peace should be living within you at all times. If you lose your peace over a word you may have heard, that could well be a sign that it isn't God speaking. I believe also that you can experience indifference, dislike or even a grieving in your spirit—further signs that we may need to detour off the path we're on. We read the other day in ***Colossians 3:15 (NLT), "let the peace that comes from Christ rule in your hearts."*** Let peace umpire your situation.

God's will may also come in the form of *the flow of the Spirit*—those times where you just sense the breath of God gently moving you in a certain direction. This can be particularly witnessed in the company of other believers. ***Acts 15:28 (NLT)*** describes a team leadership meeting where the Spirit helped them: ***"it seemed good to the Holy Spirit and to us..."***. Such a flowing will direct you, even sometimes to places that you hadn't planned. Paul experienced this on his second missionary trip. ***Acts 16:7 (NLT)*** says, ***"coming to the borders of Mysia, they headed north for the province of Bithynia, but again the Spirit of Jesus did not allow them to go there."***

Because this particular *acid test* is based on feeling emotions, we need to make sure it's God, not us. Dealing with any unconfessed sin in our life will help us make sure that we're in a good place with God, so that if we do feel something we can know it's from him. And we need to be careful that we don't let our own personal opinions and judgements stop the Spirit from flowing.

3. Is it the devil speaking?

As we saw on Day 17, the Holy Spirit can bring personal conviction in your life about various things. The Holy Spirit convicts, but the devil condemns. He may tell you to feel bad about your sin, but God says to confess it. He may tell you you're not good enough, but God says that no one is good enough. He may tell you that you're not worthy and even don't deserve to live, but we're of such value that God gave up his life so we could live in him. ***Romans 8:1 (NIVUK)*** declares, ***"There is therefore***

now no condemnation for those who are in Christ Jesus." None whatsoever. Christ dealt with every last bit on the cross.

There are always deceit and lies mixed with messages from the devil. He even tried to trick Jesus in the wilderness by quoting scripture out of context. Having taken Jesus to the highest point of the temple in ***Matthew 4:6 (NLT),*** Satan said to him, ***"If you are the Son of God, jump off! For the Scriptures say, 'He will order his angels to protect you. And they will hold you up with their hands so you won't even hurt your foot on a stone.'"*** He quoted from ***Psalm 91*** and on face value it sounds like a compelling argument. But that psalm wasn't promising a blanket prayer of safety for everyone; it was only a promise to those who were abiding and trusting in him. Therefore Jesus responded aptly in the next verse, quoting ***Deuteronomy 6:16 (NLT), "You must not test the Lord your God."*** A lie is not truth, even though it may contain things that are true.

As you practise the presence of God, these testing methods will become easier and more natural. You might think to yourself, 'What if I get it wrong?' Well, the truth is you will at some stage! But God will honour you for stepping out in faith with a desire to obey him, rather than doing nothing.

QUESTIONS TO PONDER

- **How often does scripture come to mind just when you need it? If not much, do you have at least some Bible verses committed to memory?**
- **How would you describe the difference between *God's* peace and a peaceful feeling that *you* have?**
- **Has the devil ever told you a half truth? If he has, what was it and how did you respond?**

YESTERDAY'S SUMMARY: The main way to test what we believe to be the voice of God is to see if it marries up with scripture.

DAY 42

KNOWING GOD TOGETHER

YOU MAY HAVE heard it said that going to church doesn't make you a Christian any more than going to McDonald's makes you a burger! If you haven't, it's a good one to emphasise the 'relation versus religion' aspect of Christianity that we looked at on Day 10.

But we need to be careful that we don't play down the importance of church, because if we *are* burgers then McDonald's is our home! It's where all the other burgers are. Our fast-food creator is there. It's our domain. Yes, you can now get a takeaway from the *Golden Arches*, but like watching church online it's sometimes not as warm and fresh... Let's leave the analogy there as we'll start to lose the impact. And just to say, other fast food outlets are available!

Being a Christian isn't a solo endeavour. We weren't designed to do life alone. Even the Lone Ranger had Tonto (that one may be lost on anyone under 50). We're part of the family of God, both on a global scale—the universal Church—and the neighbourhood scale—the local church. In between there are denominations and networks that enable us to do more together than any one church can do on its own. Along similar lines we see God speaking in the Bible to the global body of believers, nations, and the local church.

If we're only focused on God speaking to us individually, we're going to miss out on his big picture for our lives. Knowing God in the intimate way that we've explored throughout this book doesn't just happen on an individual level; it happens at a local church level, too. Relating to God on a personal level is one thing, but there's a *fuller* experience when we relate to him as a church.

Think, for instance, about worshipping in song. Those times when you've got the praise blasting in your car at full volume are great, but when you've got others around you, all singing together, something incredible happens. You'll understand something of this if you've ever been to a big sporting match where songs are sung by supporters. There's nothing quite like 30,000 people at the City Ground singing in unison to the tune of *Mull of Kintyre* before a kick-off. It's truly spine-tingling. Every time. Without fail. This is because God has created music to have this effect.

How much more can we sense the Spirit of God when we all channel our songs of adoration to the only one who is worthy of our praise? In those moments we truly experience a piece of heaven on earth. Our church service set lists or hymnboards aren't meant to lead us to sing nice songs to God, but to take us to mountain-top experiences where we meet with him in intimate moments that the world can't offer.

The joy of the Lord is something else that's better experienced together. I like to watch a good comedy. Watching it alone is okay, but I love to watch with other people. Why? Because there's something great about hearing other people laugh. It's infectious. But you can't laugh at your own laugh. Try it. (I know some of you just did. God knows who you are.) Now I'm not directly linking joy to happiness—happiness comes from happenings; joy comes from Jesus. But when we meet together we get to share in each other's joy, maybe through an encouragement in a small group or a testimony in a service that ripples across the congregation. ***Romans 12:15 (NIVUK)*** encourages us to ***"Rejoice with those who rejoice"***.

In ***2 John 1:12 (NLT)*** the Apostle John closes his letter with these words, ***"I have much more to say to you, but I don't want to do it with paper and ink. For I hope to visit you soon and talk with you face to face. Then our joy will be complete."*** Writing was a useful medium for John at the time. It was a joy to make contact. But communicating in person made that joy complete. I guess just like doing church online is much better than nothing; it's arguably an incomplete experience without being in the same room as everyone else.

There are other times that we can collectively enjoy intimate moments with God as a church. Think about when we might show appreciation for the preaching of God's Word, for example—it's a lot better in a room together, expressing an 'amen' or giving a clap during a sermon, than scrambling for an appropriate emoji during a live stream (and if you're watching on-demand, you don't get to share *any* feedback).

And then there's mourning. As with rejoicing, we're told to mourn with those who mourn. When someone is suffering loss, yes, you can pray for them from wherever you are—and that can help—but being with them in person to look them in the eye with compassion, having them hear the tone of your prayers, feeling the physical touch of consolation, it's all the more complete. Within this sharing of godly emotions and togetherness, the Spirit often joins in!

There's just something supernatural and powerful about being together, of one accord. We see early in the scriptures that a large group of people built the Tower of Babel. Because they were all unified in purpose and spoke the same language, they were unstoppable. ***Genesis 11:6 (NLT)*** records God's commentary on the situation. ***"'Look!' he said. 'The people are united, and they all speak the same language. After this, nothing they set out to do will be impossible for them!'"*** There was a problem though. They were using this universal principle for evil. So God had to come down and confuse their language.

It's God's intention that we all come together as one and do great exploits for *his* glory, not ours. Having my congregation all listening to different sermons online isn't a bad thing, but when we're all concentrating on the same directives and truths of God's Word at the same time it's one of the greatest superpowers on earth. Not least because Almighty God is there in the midst! This is why it's important to gather weekly to hear the shepherd's voice together or, if you can't for whatever reason, to listen back to any sermon recordings that might be available.

With all this in mind—and more (we haven't even mentioned the gifts of the Spirit, prophecy and fellowship)—it's no wonder the writer of ***Hebrews 10:24-25 (ESV)*** says, ***"let us consider how to stir up one another to love and good works, not neglecting to meet together, as is the habit of some, but encouraging one another, and all the more as you see the Day drawing near."***

So at the end of this six-week journey together, I leave you with this: don't be saved alone; don't know God alone. The devil can't take away your salvation, but if he can keep you isolated so you live a below-par Christian life he'll at least minimise the chances of others coming to Christ through you.

QUESTIONS TO PONDER

- **In what ways have you experienced God speaking to, or through, a congregation? What was the outcome?**
- **How can you play a bigger part in seeing God relating intimately with your local church? To what extent does your own attitude towards worshipping and sharing with others make a difference?**

WEEK 6 SUMMARY

Day 36: Pace Setting – Keeping with the pace of the Holy Spirit is essential for our wellbeing and spiritual productivity.

Day 37: How God Speaks – God primarily speaks to us through the Bible, so we must read this regularly to keep our relationship fresh, dynamic and productive.

Day 38: Tuning In – God is always broadcasting, but we're not always receiving.

Day 39: The Mind of Christ – When we exercise the mind of Christ we think God's thoughts and can therefore do his will.

Day 40: Fasting – Fasting minimises our dependence on the natural so as to intensify the spiritual.

Day 41: Testing the Voice of God – The main way to test what we believe to be the voice of God is to see if it marries up with scripture.

Day 42: Knowing God Together – We are created to have intimacy with God individually and corporately as a church.

The Wrap-up

FINAL THOUGHTS

I'm experiencing a tinge of nervousness in closing out this book.

As I launch out into my fourth decade of *being saved*, I look back at my life in understanding the things of God. Like many of us, in my early years of being saved I thought I knew everything—not so much out of arrogance (although that was definitely there) but because I didn't know how much there was to know! That theme stays with you throughout your years of pursuing God. On the one hand, we understand more and more; on the other hand, as we learn we're presented with even more understanding that we had no idea was there. There's always more!

So my slight reservation is knowing that once the presses are rolling and the ink is absorbed into the paper the words can't be changed. I'm not talking about a typo or any inaccurate grammar; I'm talking about the truths of God's Word. I'm talking about when in the years to come I get further revelation on a biblical truth, or understand a scripture from a new perspective, I'll wish I'd known that *now*! I doubt that I'd largely retract any part of this book, but I may present it in a different way in future. However, that's the journey of growing in God that we're all on. I just pray that you've picked up something that will move you into your next step of the great adventure in God, and that you'll ultimately experience greater intimacy with him because of it.

RECALLING THE HIGHLIGHTS

As I mentioned in the Introduction, the repetition of truths and continual building of themes throughout this book has been intentional.

Another lost art in our postmodern world of fast-paced consumerism is *meditation*. Meditation isn't just something practised by false religions (and increasingly now by atheists); it was actually God who started it all off. The opening words of the Psalms say, ***"Blessed is the one who***

does not walk in step with the wicked or stand in the way that sinners take or sit in the company of mockers, but whose delight is in the law of the Lord and who meditates on his law day and night" (Psalm 1:1-2 NIVUK). We do our best learning as human beings by means of repetition. By chewing over the same truths—like a cow chews the cud—we get further revelation, and the truth gets cemented in our brains by the creation of new neural pathways. That's the wonderful power of repetition.

With that in mind, let's summarise where we've been over the last six weeks one last time. We started in Week One by looking at our new heavenly title: *saints*. We understood that we aren't sinners but saints who sin—a seemingly subtle but important difference that positions us for intimacy. We saw how the Bible defines eternal life as *knowing God*, and that we don't have to wait for it; it's happening now. Although we're *in* the world, we're no longer *of* it; we're citizens of heaven. We established a foundational theme: that we're three-part beings. We *are* spirit, we *have* a soul, and we *live* in a body. The Spirit of God dwells inside our spirit, but there is an opposing force called the flesh (also referred to as the carnal nature, old nature, sinful capacity, or old man). Through the sacrificial work of Christ, we have the fullness of God's love and glory living inside us. We concluded by seeing that we'll end up in a new heaven on a new earth, and that we'll receive eternal rewards there based on how we live our lives *now*.

In Week Two our theme was *sanctification*—the process of becoming more holy, and how it increases our intimacy with God. We saw how we first start off our salvation as baby Christians, but God wants us to move to maturity. We established that we have the perfect *positional* righteousness of God, but are to continually grow in our *relational* righteousness with Jesus. We took a snapshot of the main world religions and saw that Christianity stands out from all of them because we worship a God who is *alive* and speaks to us. And in that relationship God is broadcasting to us 24/7, wanting to be present with us all the time. We concluded by seeing the importance of *faith* in our journey of becoming more Christ-like.

Week Three saw a gear change as we shifted our focus to *self*. Picking up on the theme of spirit, soul and body we started to understand more about the selfish, carnal side of us, which takes us away from intimacy with God. Our old ways of living are incompatible with a new life in God and can hold us back without us being aware. We saw how our free will can be used for both good and evil, and that we can't walk in the flesh and the Spirit at the same time. Even though we're new creations in Christ, we can still connect with pride—often without realising it. Then at the end of the week we established that we are born to win in life but it will sometimes be a battle, one that needs faith, the armour of God, a mind set on him, and the empowerment of the Holy Spirit.

Over halfway in, Week Four, and we explored the least favourite of the 's' words: *sin*. We saw how it creates a constant barrier between ourselves and God—not his indwelling presence (Jesus will never leave us or forsake us), but his manifest presence, the times that we strongly sense him with us in person. Sin lurks, waiting for an opportunity to enter our lives; some sins are obvious but we're blinded to others, while *not* doing what we know we should is still a sin. Then we got to the heart of the matter: we actually grieve God when we don't do what he asks of us. We took a God's-eye view that helped us see how seemingly bad situations are opportunities for us to grow in God by identifying and eliminating sin from our lives. We expanded on the latter by looking at what part both conviction and sorrow play in our lives, and how important confession and repentance are.

Week Five was all about *servanthood*, a doorway to intimacy with God. We took another look at the flesh and its similarities with the Tree of Knowledge in the Garden of Eden. We finally got to grips with another sub-theme of this book: lordship. It's a lot easier to confess Jesus as *Saviour* than *Lord*, so we explored what it means to have Jesus as Lord of our lives and how we should count the cost of following him, as well as the important part that obedience plays. We ended on two key ways to operate as servants of God: the exercising of faith through the understanding of authority, and walking in step with the Spirit of God by being yoked to the Son of God.

And in our final week we got practical as we identified some key elements of living a *Spirit-led* life. We started by seeing how God is always transmitting but we're not always receiving, and how fundamental it is that we *tune in* to hear his voice of assurance, love and instruction. We also saw how resting was vital for us to hear his voice, and how fasting turns up the volume of heaven. Understanding when God is speaking isn't always easy, so we looked at the three main ways to test words and impressions that we may receive. We ended it all by looking at the importance of knowing God *together*, particularly as a church.

WHAT NEXT?

We're all at different stages of maturity, we all have different preferences in learning styles, and we all need different things at different times. Basically, we're all different! I've not said anything new in this book, but it's still worthwhile being reminded of the truths you know and which can inspire you to keep going. Just as the Apostle Peter summarised in **2 Peter 3:1-2 (NLT), *"I have tried to stimulate your wholesome thinking and refresh your memory. I want you to remember what the holy prophets said long ago and what our Lord and Savior commanded through your apostles."***

Some of the themes in this book may have sparked a desire in you to find out more. We've just skimmed the surface of the focus presented on each day, but every one of them could merit its own book! The intention here is certainly not meant to be exhaustive but to make sure we cover as many as possible of the everyday themes in our journeys of *being saved*. That in turn brings us closer to God. If you're like me and love to go deeper, then make sure you do. This book is like a big bunch of keys; all I'm doing is presenting different ones to you and doing my best to give you an overview of the room that it leads you into. Go and explore!

It may be that you're a relatively new Christian, or perhaps you've been going to church for years but a fair bit of what you've read is new to you. If that's you, my strong advice is simple: read this book again! Whether it's one day at a time, all at once or just revisiting the parts that quizzed you the most, the more you revisit the more cemented the truths become. (I think the most reads of a single book I've done is four times!) And revisit the questions, too. You might be in a different place when you read them again; you might think different thoughts; God may prompt you in different ways. You might only be one step away from breakthrough in your life, but you have to hear from God to understand what that step is.

TAKING ACTION

We must also remember that ***James 2:20 (NLT)*** says, ***"How foolish! Can't you see that faith without good deeds is useless?"*** Mere head knowledge doesn't do anything in the Kingdom. It's only the transference into *action* that achieves anything of value.

So here's a list of practical steps that you could consider putting into action right now. Read them slowly. Give the Holy Spirit a chance to highlight anything in particular. All of them will better your experience of *being saved.*

- **Schedule in daily time with God.** Start small if you have to. Ten minutes is infinitely better than nothing.
- **Set an 'activity trigger' that reminds you to focus on God.** Maybe it's a commute, a dog walk, or just when you're brushing your teeth.
- **Hook up with a mentor or accountability partner.** Give someone permission to speak into your life if they see you acting 'worldly'.
- **Pray daily confessions.** Whether part of a morning quiet time or as your head hits the pillow at night, fit this in somewhere to make sure the lines of communication are fully open between you and God.
- **Repent.** Ask God to reveal any area of your life that isn't under the lordship of Christ. Habitual sin is an indicator. Dig out the root.

- **Forgive.** Scan your heart for anyone's face that might pop up relating to an offence. This is too serious to try and justify holding on to. Let it go now!
- **Commit to regular fellowship.** We were created to do life together. Make sure you're gathering with your local church whenever you can, at least once a week if possible. Prioritise it.
- **Do life in a smaller group.** Build a relationship with a small group of believers where you can interact more intimately.
- **Serve God.** Whether it's general work that needs to be done or something that utilises your gifts and personality—ideally both—make yourself available.
- **Take communion outside of a church service.** Acknowledge the presence of God around the dinner table, and when dining out with other believers.
- **Review your life connections.** Do you need more Christian friends? Are there carnal people in your life who potentially lead you astray?
- **Be filled with the Spirit.** If you've never been filled before, ask God to baptise you now. If you have, ask again for a top up—daily.
- **Fast.** Add fasting to your prayers to reach levels of intimacy with God that you've never experienced before. Commit regularly if you can, maybe weekly or monthly.
- **Practise obedience.** Sit with God for a few minutes and ask him what he wants you to do. It may be big or small. Follow the process of testing his voice if necessary.
- **Study an area of this book**—maybe one of the daily focuses or sections. Google the subject. Buy a book on it. Watch a YouTube video about it. Discuss it with a friend. Go deeper.
- **Put on some worship music.** Bang it on in the car, whilst you're walking or quietly in bed as you're settling. Whenever you do it,

focus on the truth of the lyrics at the same time as listening to the melody. Lift God up to his rightful place.

- **Invite a friend to church.** It's good to share the gospel with friends and family, but when you bring them to a church gathering they get to experience the unity of the Spirit in action. That's powerful.

CONCLUDING PRAYER

Allow me to pray one last time as we run past the finishing line together:

"Lord God, you see each person reading these words. You see both their outer circumstances and their inner thoughts. You know where they are spiritually. You see the battles within that no one else sees—looking at them in perfect detail with total clarity. You know what the next step for them is. I'm not with them to counsel them personally, but you are, and you're inside them, moving now even as this prayer registers with their heart.

"Stir that heart, Lord. Do it now. Stimulate a desire for more of you. Develop a need for holiness. Ignite a passion for your presence. Flood their souls with your love and mercy. Send a shockwave of Kingdom power into the core of their being. Do what only you can do, bringing wholeness into their lives. Where there is hurt, minister healing; where there is lack, send your word; where there is despair, administer hope.

"Finally, I speak to every power of darkness that stands in the way of their spiritual progress and command you to leave. I rebuke you in the name of Jesus, and stand with God's precious child in declaring that Jesus is Lord!

"Your Kingdom come, Lord, your will be done. Amen."

APPENDIX

The Glossary

FOR THOSE WHO are relatively new to the faith or aren't quite sure what some of the words mentioned in the book actually mean, I've put together this list of definitions. I've tried to steer away from theological terms as best I can, and have attempted to explain things in everyday language.

- **Apostle:** A father in the faith. In the specific sense: the twelve disciples of Jesus. In the general sense: a person who is sent out to establish and strengthen churches, and preach the gospel.

- **Born again:** The birthing of your spirit, which previously lay in an unconscious state. It's the start of being a 'new creation' in Christ. You were once born a physical being *without* a spirit, then you became a spiritual being *with* a body.

- **Carnal:** Acts of the flesh (see "**Flesh**").

- **Church:** Although often associated with a building, *church* is actually the people who meet in it. More accurately, it's those who have been called out by God. The word can be referenced in relation to a specific local church, or a network of churches, and also the global 'one' Church of Jesus Christ.

- **Christ** (also **Messiah**)**:** A title of Jesus that literally means *Anointed One* or *Chosen One*, and is the Greek equivalent of the word *Messiah*.

- **Communion** (also **The Lord's Table/Supper** or **Eucharist**)**:** An ordinance started by Jesus around a meal table where he shared bread and wine with his disciples as symbols of his broken body and shed blood, respectively. He instructs us to continue with this practice so we can remember his life, his sacrifice that brought in the new covenant and his return for us, his Church.

- **Confess:** In terms of salvation, it means to *announce your faith in Christ* for the forgiveness of sin that gives you access to God's Kingdom; in terms of everyday life, it means to *admit your sin* and receive the forgiveness that gives you access to his manifest presence.

- **Covenant** (also **Testament**): An agreement between God and man that involves promises—the Old and New Testaments being the major covenants in the Bible.

- **Denomination:** A group of churches that believe things slightly differently from other Christian groups. However, all true Christian denominations agree that the Lord Jesus Christ is God, who became a man in order to die for our sins, and that faith in him and his resurrection is the only way to receive eternal life.

- **Disciple:** A Christian, someone who believes in and follows (obeys) the teachings of the Lord Jesus Christ. It started with 12; now we're part of millions worldwide.

- **Fellowship:** The social intercourse we have with other Christians through the shared experience of being saved. It goes far deeper than friendship or other human relationships. It includes mutual encouragement, love and a unity in purpose and spirit. We also experience fellowship with Christ when we confess our sins (this relates to **Communion**, above).

- **Flesh** (also **Carnal**): Our sinful desires, temptations and lusts that dwell in our human nature. It's the source of temptation, and nothing good dwells there. (The term *flesh* can also refer to humankind, or our physical bodies—more so in the Old Testament—but is predominantly used in this book as meaning our human nature.)

- **Glorification:** Just as we received new *spiritual* life when we got saved, we will receive new *physical* life when we receive our new glorified bodies at Jesus' return. What this will look like we don't fully know, but we do have at least some indication from the times Jesus appears in his new resurrection body at the beginning of the book of Acts.

- **Glory:** A multi-faceted word that describes God's manifest presence; it indicates worth and value which results in praise. It's also a synonym for heaven. We can reflect Christ's glory, just as Jesus reflected the glory of his Father in heaven.

- **Gospel:** Meaning *good news*, specifically the good news of Jesus' life, death and resurrection for our salvation, healing and provision, and the hope of eternal life that Jesus made available to us by God's grace.

- **Grace:** God's undeserved favour that gives us eternal life, as well as empowering us to live it.

- **Holy** (also **Sanctified**): To be holy means to be separate, different or set apart. On one level all Christians are holy, in the sense that God has set us apart for his purposes and for his glory. On another level we're all called to be holy in our conduct (also known as *sanctification*). This is the theme that runs right the way through this book.

- **Justification:** The act of all our sins being forgiven and washed away from us forever. This takes place at the very moment we receive Jesus Christ into our lives as Lord and Saviour. Someone once said, "When I am justified, it's 'just-as-if-I'd' never sinned!" The result is that we receive the righteousness of Christ.

- **Kingdom of God** (also **Kingdom of Heaven**)**:** God's rule and reign, especially that which is now extended through the earth, instigated by Christ's sacrificial death on the cross.

- **Lordship of Christ:** Refers to the fact that Jesus Christ is totally in command of our lives. He's the King. He gives us orders and commands that we obey. He's our Master. When we receive Jesus Christ into our lives, we receive him as both Saviour and Lord.

- **Lost:** The term used for people who have not come into a relationship with God through Jesus Christ.

- **Messiah:** Literally *Chosen One* or *Anointed One*; the Hebrew equivalent of Christ.

- **Pharisee:** A group of extremely devout Jews who were intent on obeying the Laws of Moses to the *nth* degree. Their error was in totally missing the *spirit* the laws were given in.

- **Prophecy:** At its core, a message of encouragement from God. In its more nuanced delivery, a specific message of direction for an individual, church or even nation. (If you prophesy—which we're all encouraged to do—it doesn't make you a prophet. See below.)

- **Prophet:** A messenger from God. One of the five 'offices' of God found in Ephesians 4:11. A person is only considered a prophet if their prophecy is true and consistent with God and his word.

- **Rabbi:** A Jewish teacher.

- **Repent:** To change your mind and heart completely about sin and ultimately to walk away from it, as in 'do a 180'. We repent initially at the point of salvation, then at times in our life when we have got ourselves into habitual sin that requires a recognition of what we have been doing, whilst asking God to remove our desire for it.

- **Revelation:** As well as being the name of the last book of the Bible, it also refers to an *unveiling* concerning scripture—the revealing of God's Word about himself and his plan of salvation for the world.

- **Righteousness:** Right standing with God. Positionally, we are 100 per cent righteous, perfect in his eyes. Relationally, we grow in righteousness (see **Sanctification**).

- **Sabbath:** To stop. Rest. Down tools. A time also to separate for worshipping God. It's a 24-hour period, normally observed in the western world every Sunday, but can actually be any day of the week.

- **Sacrifice:** In the Old Testament animal sacrifices were offered up to God as a substitute for our sin. Now, in the New Testament, our life in Christ should be offered to God as a 'living sacrifice'. Within that, God may ask us to give up things that are valuable to us, not just as an act of obedience and worship to him, but also to benefit others.

- **Saints:** In its most basic sense, a saint is a *holy one,* someone who is set apart for God's special purposes. As a result every follower of Jesus Christ is a saint. (See also **Holy.**)

- **Salvation** (also *having been saved*): The fact that God has rescued, or saved, us from our sins and from the consequences of sin (death) and the wrath of God. In the Bible we see three aspects of salvation—*justification* (having been saved), *sanctification* (being saved), and *glorification* (yet to be saved).

- **Sanctified** (also **Sanctification**: see **Holy**)

- **Second Coming** (also **Return of Christ**): The physical return of Jesus Christ to earth, with the armies of heaven at his side, to judge his enemies, set up his kingdom and fulfill the prophecies to Israel.

- **Sin:** Akin to *missing the mark*. It's when we go against the will and instructions of God through what we do or don't do, in thought, word or deed.

- **Soul:** The invisible part of you (along with your spirit) that contains your mind, will and emotions. In essence, it's what makes you a spiritual being.

- **Sovereignty:** God's complete control over all things in nature and the affairs of men. The choices we make are weaved into that on the basis that he knows all things—past, present, and future—and is both inside and outside time.

- **Trinity:** The one and only true God existing as three persons: God the Father, God the Son (Jesus), and God the Spirit (Holy Spirit). It's a hard one to grasp with our minds, but if we think that water has three forms—water, steam and ice—it helps, in some small way at least, to start getting our heads around it. (Interestingly, you won't find the word *Trinity* in the Bible!)

- **The World:** This can refer to different aspects in the Bible, such as the physical world and the human world, but in this book it's mainly used to describe the moral world. The world in that sense includes unsaved people, the God-hostile environment they conform to and, in the widest sense, corruption and evil. *Worldly* describes behaviour and attitudes that occur outside a knowledge of God. (See also **Carnal**.)

- **Worship:** Reverence and devotion toward God alone. Although it's most commonly associated with times of singing our praises to God, it's actually more than that. Much more. We worship God by the way we live our life in his name, by giving him all glory and honour.

The Journalling Pages

SOME YEARS AGO I developed a system to help people who weren't great at having a daily devotional time with God. Truth be known, it was first and foremost for myself!

Whereas Kate has always been incredibly well disciplined in this area, I've been left lacking too often. I don't know about you, but I've not always been great at slowing down and being still. I always felt I wasn't hearing God as much as I could in my 'quiet times'—which weren't even that consistent.

For many of us who are struggling to grow in this area of Christian life, it's partly down to pressing into God and practising being in his presence. But for some of us it's also about the way we're wired. If you're like me, you love structure. Many people think that God is restricted by structure, but actually he happily moves within it. Just as a river flows with the aid of its banks, so too the Spirit can move through a structured approach to spending dedicated time with him.

Having found greater joy in spending time with God through the system I developed, I asked others to try it too. The feedback was very positive, and resulted in me producing journals based around the system.

Overleaf you'll see a copy of the journal pages that guide you through a devotional time with God each day. Feel free to use this system or even copy the pages so you can try it for yourself. If you turn the page again you'll see a list of instructions that explain how to go through each step and get the most out of it all.

This isn't for everyone, but if you find it helps you then you can purchase a journal at www.journaljunkies.co.uk.

However you choose to be alone with the Lord, my plea to you is that you make sure to prioritise it, for it's in these times that we develop our relationship with God. It's the only way that we can grow in intimacy with him.

Day: Date: Month:

1. THANKS:

2. PRAISE:

3. CONFESS:

4. READ: BIBLE REFERENCE:

SCRIPTURE:

5. THINK:

'THINK' CONTINUED:

6. ACT:

7. PRAY:

ADDITIONAL/OVERFLOW NOTES:

How to use the daily journalling pages

1. THANKS

Having an attitude of gratitude is always the best way to start your devotional time with God. Thanksgiving opens the door to his presence. At this point you write down one thing that, over the last 24 hours, has been a blessing to you. It may be something natural or spiritual, it may seem big or small; that doesn't matter. What matters is that you start appropriately. ***Psalm 100:4 (NIVUK)*** says, ***"Enter his gates with thanksgiving and his courts with praise; give thanks to him and praise his name".*** Take a few minutes to think more about what you've written and thank God in the process.

2. PRAISE

Whereas thanksgiving gets you into his presence, praise positions you there. ***Psalm 113:1 (NIVUK)*** says, ***"Praise the name of the LORD."*** After thanking him for *what he's done*, you now spend a few minutes praising him for *who he is*. Think about one of God's many wonderful attributes, and write it in the space provided. You could also put on some worship music at this time to help you express your praise to him.

3. CONFESS

Jesus took the punishment for your sins on the cross once and for all time. So the penalty for every wrong you've done—whether past, present or future—has been dealt with, but the effects of sin can still hamper your everyday walk with God. That's where confession comes in. At this point you write down a short prayer of confession, asking for forgiveness. In addition, you may want to take a few moments to reflect and ask the Holy Spirit to reveal any situations that you need to confess and put right, whether it's a wrong that you've said or done to other people, or things that you *should* have said or done, but didn't. Furthermore, you may want to confess certain sins to a trusted Christian friend. Or you may need to ask for forgiveness from someone you have wronged. Let the Holy Spirit lead you, as King David did in ***Psalms 139:23-24 (NLT), "Search me, O God, and know my heart; test me and know my anxious thoughts. Point out anything in me that offends you, and lead me along the path of everlasting life."***

4. READ

This is your daily bread! ***Matthew 4:4 (NIVUK)*** says, ***"Man shall not live on bread alone, but on every word that comes from the mouth of God."*** The Bible is your instructional manual for life—God-breathed words that will nourish your spirit, soul and body. As you read the scriptures you're looking to identify just *one* verse, concept or idea that stands out to you, whether interesting or poignant, Holy Spirit-inspired or just different. Use a reading plan each day and ask the Holy Spirit to help you find your 'highlighted' verse as you read. When you get it, simply enter that scripture reference and write the verse out in full. If you find that several verses stick out, highlight or underline them in your Bible or note them down, then when you've finished reading select just one. It doesn't matter which one you choose if you're unsure.

5. THINK

This is an important part of the process. It's where you meditate on the verse or theme you've chosen, chewing it over in your mind. ***Psalm 34:8 (NIVUK)*** says, ***"Taste and see that the Lord is good".*** The Holy Spirit will reveal things to you as you stop and think. Observe in more detail what your focus means to you (not necessarily what the Bible commentators say, or what the devotional writers say, but what *you* say). What is interesting, different, unusual or revealing about it? In the space provided, write down a summary of what you've considered. You could also try reading Bible study notes, or read your focus verse from an alternative translation and/or paraphrase to get a fuller picture of what God is saying.

6. ACT

Reading scripture is not enough; meditating on it is a step in the right direction, but acting on it is nothing short of what God wants us to do. So think about how this focus applies to you: how will you be different today as a result of what you've just read? Write down a summary of how you can personally respond to God's Word, because ***James 1:23-34 (NIVUK)*** says, ***"Anyone who listens to the word but does not do what it says is like a man who looks at his face in a mirror and, after looking at himself, goes away and immediately forgets what he looks like."***

7. PRAY

Seal this time in prayer, committing your ways to God as you have been led through the process. Write out a short prayer in the space provided. You can then use this as a launch pad to continue with other prayers you have in mind. Be assured that God hears your prayers when you're in good standing with him—with no unconfessed sin holding you back. ***1 John 5:14-15 (NLT)*** says, ***"And we are confident that he hears us whenever we ask for anything that pleases him. And since we know he hears us when we make our requests, we also know that he will give us what we ask for."***